The World Trading System at Risk

The World Trading
System at Risk

Jagdish Bhagwati

PRINCETON UNIVERSITY PRESS

PRINCETON, NEW JERSEY

Library of Congress Cataloging-in-Publication Data
Bhagwati, Jagdish N.
The world trading system at risk / Jagdish Bhagwati.
p.   cm.
Based on the author's Harry Johnson memorial lecture, delivered at the Royal Society of Arts in London on July 11, 1990.
Sequel to: Protectionism (1988)
Includes bibliographical references.
ISBN 0-691-04284-5
1. General Agreement on Tariff and Trade (Organization)   2. Uruguay Round (1987–)   3. International trade.   I. Title.
HF1711.B45   1991   382'.92—dc20   90-21389

This book has been composed in Adobe Palatino

Princeton University Press books are printed on acid-free paper, and meet the guidelines for permanence and durability of the Committee on Production Guidelines for Book Longevity of the Council on Library Resources

Printed in the United States of America by Princeton University Press, Princeton, New Jersey

10 9 8 7 6 5 4 3 2 1

Contents

Preface

HARRY JOHNSON passed away on May 9, 1977. At fifty-three, he died prematurely, a stroke ending a life of remarkable accomplishment that led the Nobel laureate James Tobin to declare ours as the Age of Johnson. But, as if by providential design, he died in Geneva: the home of the General Agreement on Tariffs and Trade, the anchor of the postwar trading system, whose design his scientific and policy writings ceaselessly explored, but whose importance he never doubted, and whose redesign at the Uruguay Round and beyond is the great task now before us.

Nothing would then have been more appropriate on the occasion of celebrating his life and his work than to consider the prospects for the GATT-focused multilateral trading system. This volume, growing out of the Harry Johnson Memorial Lecture delivered at the Royal Society of Arts in London on July 11, 1990, does precisely that.

The broad sweep of the scientific and policy issues that I must offer to do justice to this subject puts me in debt to the contributions and insights of many more than the few whom I have cited. But I must not forget to say that my greatest indebtedness is to Harry Johnson himself. A towering presence, a charismatic lecturer, unfailing in his generosity, he remains among my most memorable teachers at Cambridge, and his work in international economics remains the foundation on which we all have continued to build.

I should like to thank Hugh Corbet and the Harry G. Johnson Memorial Committee for the gracious hospitality extended to me during my visit to London. I am

vii

also happy to acknowledge the congenial and intellectually stimulating environment of the National Bureau of Economic Research where the manuscript was finished for publication.

James Benedict, Donald Davis, and Margaret Pasquale provided excellent research assistance. I owe them special thanks.

August 1990
Jagdish Bhagwati

The World Trading System at Risk

CHAPTER ONE

Overview

THE MULTILATERAL trading system, focused on the General Agreement on Tariffs and Trade (GATT), is at a crossroads.* The threats presently faced by the GATT arise from a variety of fundamental changes in the world economy. These changes have produced fissiparous tendencies gnawing at many of the basic principles embodied in the GATT.

Recalling that the preamble to the GATT forcefully declares its objective as the pursuit of "reciprocal and mutually advantageous arrangements directed to the substantial reduction of tariffs and other barriers to trade and to the elimination of discriminatory treatment in international commerce," and mindful of its central articles, I may justifiably cite the following as the principal principles of the GATT:

1. A "fix-rule" trading regime is to be preferred to a "fix-quantity" one. Equivalently, "managed trade" (or

---

* The GATT is the main institution overseeing world trade today. The 1944 Bretton Woods conference, which established the charters of the International Monetary Fund and the World Bank, was not concerned with trade, although the importance of a comparable institution for trade was recognized at it. The United States later published a draft charter for the International Trade Organization in 1946, but this came to naught in the end. Instead, the negotiated multilateral agreement to reduce tariffs reciprocally, along with a draft of the general clauses of obligations relating to the tariff obligations, became the GATT. It was completed by October 1947 and brought into effect by the adoption of the "Protocol of Provisional Application," which would then be applied by twenty-three nations. For an invaluable, brief but succinct history, see Jackson (1990, ch. 1).

its populist version, "results-oriented" trade), which seeks quantitative targets of outcomes in trade instead of settling on rules and letting the chips fall where they may, is to be rejected.

2. Multilateralism, where these trade rules[1] extend without discrimination to all members of the trading regime, is generally to be preferred to discriminatory arrangements.

3. Markets are to be opened through conventional reduction in trade barriers, and new disciplines are to be established, by resort to mutuality and balance of concessions. The trade concessions thus are to be traded on the basis of what can be called "first-difference" reciprocity, that is, *changes* in barriers are to be balanced in the negotiations. The *overall* reciprocity of openness presumably follows because, when members join, their "price" of membership includes the agreed-upon leveling of trade barriers that would implicitly establish initial balance of barriers between the new and the old members.[2] This rules out unilaterally determined demands for unrequited concessions that could come from the strong against the weak.[3] Equivalently, the rule of law is to prevail in negotiations toward freer trade, not the law of the jungle.

4. In the same spirit of the rule of law, the adjudication of disputes must be impartial, pitting the strong against the weak in equal contest, with both the balance of negotiations and the impartiality of dispute settlement reflecting the correct and growing perception that the GATT system is the best defense of the weak.

Permit me at the outset to consider and dismiss two wholly different sets of skepticism directed at the GATT and these principles. One comes from the scholarly direction; the other is frivolous but, reflecting the force of Gresham's law, the more pervasive. Take each, in turn.

Ingenious economists properly make their mark by proving the improbable. "Paradox gained" translates swiftly into success and professional reward. The scientific game continues relentlessly into "paradox lost," then "paradox regained," and then on in cycles that leave residues of added insights into the phenomena we seek to understand and the policies we hope to define.

But in making policy, scientific ingenuity must blend with good sense. Sir Dennis Robertson, the great Cambridge economist, once aptly described a brilliant young economist who had wandered into the policy arena as "silly-clever." Silliness from clever economists does afflict the debate on GATT principles. Thus, clever examples of national gains from discrimination, as in selectivity in the use of safeguards or in preferential tariff cuts only among a few, can certainly be constructed under certain specific assumptions. Indeed, they are routinely taught in our classrooms. But for policy, we must ask: Are those assumptions sensible? which model among the many is appropriate to the problem at hand? We must cut through the exotic underbrush to the path that leads through the forest. The principles of the GATT define that path.

But if scholarly qualifications must be judged in perspective, the frivolous criticisms recently directed at the GATT must be put in their place. A common criticism is that the GATT is in truth the General Agreement to Talk and Talk: It has delivered nothing. This is nonsense. Under GATT auspices, tariff barriers of the OECD countries went down to almost negligible levels; the Tokyo Round then began the assault on

nontariff barriers in a process that is now being pur-
sued further, along with the task of extending GATT
discipline to new sectors, at the Uruguay Round.

The facile views of GATT's impotence are fashion-
able in the United States among several lobbies and in
Congress. They principally reflect panic at the payments deficit and at the rise of Japan. Quick fixes on
the trade front, using American muscle to extract
trade concessions unilaterally and quickly from others, regardless of the impact on the world trading
regime, therefore have a superficial but compelling
appeal.

But, alas, ignorant prattle by academic economists
has also fueled these sentiments. Unburdened by historical knowledge, scientific expertise, and the sustained scholarly reflection that these matters require
and that the lay public automatically arrogates to
them in view of either their distinction in fields other
than international trade or their public visibility, these
economists have entered trade policy with pronouncements that will not survive scrutiny but which nonetheless bring comfort to the political forces and the economic interests that see no virtue in the GATT and its
tenets. Nothing is more important to special interests
than to seek legitimacy by citing at least "one reputa-
ble academic" on their side so that the congruence of
their private gain and the public good is established.

The United States thus has been witness currently,
for instance, to economists (in full flight as instant converts to trade expertise) turning on the GATT with
criticisms that betray ignorance of the institution and
its functioning,* advocating "managed trade" in the

---

* See the expose of errors regarding the GATT in Rudiger Dornbusch et al. (1989), a pamphlet written for Eastman Kodak Com-

shape of imposing quantitative targets for imports of manufactures on Japan, recommending GATT-illegal tariff retribution (unmindful of treaty obligations and systemic implications for the GATT and the Uruguay Round) in case such targets on imports are not fulfilled (Dornbusch 1989), and the like. Such forays into unfamiliar territory certainly get one a place in the sun—but the sun can scorch, too. I think it is fair to say, as would have Harry Johnson who denied the benefit of his biting sarcasm to none who deserved it, that the exposure of incompetence in these matters has been its own punishment, and the GATT's supporters need fear no serious threat from this quarter.

But my good friend Lester Thurow, with his famous, or shall I say infamous, announcement at the 1988 Davos Symposium that the "GATT is dead," is another matter. His prominence, sustained interest in public policy, and role as the new intellectual force in Democratic circles lend his pronouncements special importance. But Thurow is dead wrong. While I return to his views later, a brief response should suffice presently.

For an institution whose irrelevance is implied by Thurow's claim to have discovered the corpse, it is remarkable that since 1982, the number of contracting parties (as the GATT members are technically described) has risen by 12 percent from eighty-six to ninety-six. Currently, eight more countries are negotiating their accession, China is negotiating its status, and the Soviet Union is waiting eagerly in the wings.

---

pany, by Michael Finger (1989). Many of these fallacies are discussed in Appendix I, which also extends to the clarification of the confused and sloppy usage of key concepts that is now plaguing the discussion of trade policy.

Surely, necrophilia has not broken out! The rush to membership is an adequate riposte to Thurow: A feast attracts people more readily than a funeral.

Then again, the number of dispute settlement cases coming to the GATT has risen significantly in recent years (as is manifest from the tabulation in Appendix III), testifying to the growing importance of the institution in a role that had fallen into virtual oblivion through disuse earlier. Yet another index of GATT's continued vitality and increasing importance is the growth in the number of countries, and in the value of trade covered, in the successive rounds of trade negotiations, from the earliest Geneva Round in 1947 to the Tokyo Round in 1973–1979 and on to the current Uruguay Round (as is evident from Table 1).

But the decisive answer to Thurow's fears can be given by reminding him—an American, an ex-colonial like me (an Indian) of her Majesty's erstwhile empire—that when the monarch dies, the British say: The Queen is dead; long live the Queen. The GATT certainly is, in some key respects, in need of repair and

TABLE 1
GATT Negotiating Rounds

Round	Dates	Number of Countries	Value of Trade Covered (dollars)
Geneva	1947	23	10 billion
Annecy	1949	33	Unavailable
Torquay	1950	34	Unavailable
Geneva	1956	22	2.5 billion
Dillon	1961	45	4.9 billion
Kennedy	1962	48	40 billion
Tokyo	1973	99	155 billion

Source: Jackson 1990, 37.

8

reconstruction to profit from four decades of experience and to accommodate the needs of a changed world economy. But that is precisely what the Uruguay Round is about. So, my response to Thurow is: The GATT is dead; long live the GATT.

But the success of the Uruguay Round is not guaranteed. As the contracting parties enter the last lap of this arduous race, heading towards Brussels in December 1990, deeply troubling questions arise as to the feasibility of a successful bargain among them. The necessity of achieving success is evident; but the nature of the deal defining that success is not. Though there is an abundance of advice on the dimensions of a deal, I am prompted to offer somewhat different, and I should hope, fruitful ideas on how the final negotiations might successfully conclude.

But before I do that, I must turn to the rather serious challenges to the GATT principles of multilateralism and its corollaries that have recently arisen from several directions and taken the form of an advocacy of managed trade, aggressive unilateralism, and regionalism. Underlying these phenomena, though deriving strength also from other factors, is a common thread: the increasing sensitivity to "unfair trade" and the sense that the methods of the GATT-based multilateral trading system cannot cope with the issues that unfair trade by one's rivals forces on our attention.

PART ONE

THE GATT ARCHITECTURE:
THE THREAT

CHAPTER TWO

The Rise of Unfair Trade

WHY HAVE concerns about unfair trade risen to the forefront today? A conjunction of several factors drives these concerns.

But if these forces have to be understood, assessed, and, for the most part, declared as hazardous to the health of the world trading regime, it is necessary to analyze the role of free trade vis-à-vis fair trade.

Fair trade plays no role in the economic tradition, dating back to the British policy during the latter half of the nineteenth century, that emphasizes that unilateral free trade is advantageous for oneself no matter what others do. The "strategic" notion that if your trading partner has trade barriers while you don't, you might be able to use retaliatory tariffs and the like to force down those barriers and gain twice over from free trade—once from your own, then from hers—was known to both Adam Smith and Alfred Marshall. It was also dismissed by them as either inapplicable (for Britain) or unwise or both. But it is certainly not an argument based on the notion that your trading partner's tariffs and trade barriers are "unfair."

But one can take an alternative, cosmopolitan or systemic approach to free trade that yields a different answer. One can argue that a free trade *regime* (such as the GATT), overseeing trade among trading nations, must embody the principle of symmetrical free trade by each;[1] otherwise, the efficient allocation of activity among trading nations that the regime must reflect will be compromised by the license taken by those who stray.

There is also the prudential argument that, even if one were not interested in cosmopolitanism and were actuated only by considerations of narrow national interest, one's own ability to sustain free trade would be imperiled in practice if one's rivals were considered to be trading unfairly, as when they deeply subsidize their firms, which then elbow one's own firms out of the marketplace despite lack of "true" advantage in efficiency. Pluralist politics will generally rule out accommodation to free trade unless trade is also seen to be fair.

Hence, historically, the liberalization of trade, as in the aftermath of the disastrous Smoot-Hawley tariff of 1930, or currently in the developing countries that dismantle trade barriers under World Bank conditionality, has been accompanied by the institution or activation of the two now-conventional fair trade mechanisms: the countervailing duty (CVD) against foreign subsidization of exports and the antidumping (AD) duty to counteract the presumably predatory effects of dumping.

The problem is that fair trade is a two-faced creature: One face is friendly to free trade; the other frowns on it, indeed, seeks to devour it, for fair trade mechanisms can be misused to allege unfair trade unfairly and thus undermine free trade. And new definitions of widening scope, of what constitutes unfair, "unreasonable," unacceptable trade, can be invented in unending improvisations. It is this other, ugly face, with its wide and menacing grin reminiscent of Jack Nicholson in his more villainous roles, that we presently see and must fear. Why?

1. Perhaps the most compelling reason for the rise of unfair trade allegations is simply the outbreak of protectionist pressures in the early 1980s in the after-

math of the second oil shock and the worldwide recession that Paul Volcker instituted to wring inflation out of the world economy.

Academic economists now distinguish between the supply of protection by governments and the demand for it by its beneficiaries, often the corporate and labor interests. In the OECD countries, with some variations, the governments have been generally skeptical of protectionism, and those who demand protection must generally wrest it from reluctant governments. Need it be doubted then that protection is easier to procure if the successful foreign rival is alleged to be unfairly trading than if one pleads for it merely by citing the difficulty of one's situation?

2. But if the allegations of unfair trade can become the handmaiden of protectionism, the implausibility with which such allegations can be made by protectionists is diminished by the increased focus on non-tariff barriers (NTBs) relative to the now-negligible tariffs. The latter are transparent and indeed uncomplicated. Gertrude Stein could have said: A tariff is a tariff is a tariff. But NTBs are hard to handle. Suspicions often linger of their invisible hand strangulating trade. The Japan-bashers prosper on the allegations, as hard to disprove as they are easy to make, that Japan's invisible barriers keep out imports, frustrating other nations' trading access and nullifying their trading rights.

3. But, in addition to these reasons for the appeal of unfair trade allegations to those who seek to moderate the force of competition in trade, there are also changes in the world economy that reinforce the move of unfair trade concerns to center stage.

Perhaps the most important factor, responsible in particular for the American conversion to neurosis on

15

this front, has been the relative decline of the United States within the world economy, leading to what I christened some years ago the diminished giant syndrome.[2]

The diminished giant syndrome of the United States now parallels the one of Britain at the end of the nineteenth century, when the United States and Germany arrived on the world scene: In each case, concerns with the trading success of the newly triumphant countries became the order of the day. "Fair trade" and "reciprocity" were the buzz words in Britain then, as they are in the United States now.

But the panic, and the petulance about the rivals, have an extra edge in the United States today. The psychological need to be "number one" is evidently more compelling in a country where there is ceaseless ranking of institutions, corporations, the sartorially elegant, and the wealthiest. And then again, the country whose rise promotes the challenge, Japan, is one that is peculiarly susceptible to charges of unfair trade. Indeed, such allegations against Japan have been so common for at least half a century that I have suggested that today's Japan-bashers, in reviving old and fearful stereotypes about Japan, should be called regressionists rather than the revisionists they fancy themselves to be.

4. But the change in the world economy that propels more forcefully the unfair trade crusade is the increased crisscrossing of foreign investments, with associated dramatic increases in trade-to-GNP ratios of many countries, which is turning the globalized world economy into a veritable spider's web.

This "spider's web" phenomenon has meant increasingly that everyone tends now to be in everyone else's backyard, making import competition in one's own market, and export competition in the other's market and in third markets, ever more fierce. In this atmosphere, reminiscent of the struggle for the sun in a dense tropical forest, suspicions of unfair advantage accruing to one's rivals arise readily and fester and then poison the political process that makes trade policy.

5. But yet another aspect of the world economy, the arrival of flexible exchange rates, has also added to the problem. Volatility in the exchange rate can wipe you out and your only recourse may be to cry "foul"; the rival who gains from the changed rate is not going to complain, leaving the floor to those who lose.

Dramatic shifts in rates, such as the yen-dollar rate before and after the 1985 Plaza Accord, underline the intensity of the problem that can arise. I think it is pretty obvious that unless some degree of stability in the structure of exchange rates is achieved by coordination of underlying macroeconomic policies, the rise of unfair trade allegations will be hard to contain and will lead to demands for a fix-quantity rather than a fix-rule trading regime. The choice in practice may well be between managed exchange rates and managed trade.

6. But an important role in making unfair trade concerns potent in politics has also been played by developments in the realm of ideas and ideology. In the conventional analyses of commercial policy, the tradition was that in cases such as infant industry protection, properly identified and then legitimately granted, there would be *irreversible* gains in efficiency and competitiveness in the industry so protected. But when foreign countries so intervened, this was treated as unobjectionable even though it would, *ceteris paribus*, harm one's own industry and even damage one's eco-

17

nomic welfare. Indeed, Alfred Marshall, during Britain's debate on fair trade and reciprocity at the end of the nineteenth century, argued explicitly for indulgence towards others' infant industry tariffs.

In the theoretical models that have recently been analyzed, with oligopolistic competition among competing firms from different nations formally modeled, the irreversibility of gains from scale economies plays a similar role, but the context within which it does so is less benign than in the conventional infant industry case. For instance, assume that all firms are otherwise identical, the Japanese market is closed to the American firm but the American market is open to the Japanese firm, and scale economies are irreversible (that is, once you experience them, they stay with you, as when learning follows from doing). Then it is evident that the Japanese firm has two markets, while the American firm has only one, so the Japanese firm will wipe out the American firm. Not merely would the industry be lost; even economic well-being may be damaged.[3] The probability of damage to economic well-being increases if having the industry within one's borders would have produced external economies for oneself.* What such models demonstrate is that the most improbable and negligible-looking form of unfair advantage provided by foreign governments can lead to predatory and large effects on one's industry's competitiveness and survival, and on one's welfare.

The loss of a few high-tech industries to Japan, the visibility of some Japanese governmental support and the assumed presence of invisible support in myriad

---

* External economies may obtain across borders too, as in the case of environmental pollution. When they do, the geographical location of the external-economies-bearing industry becomes a lesser issue.

18

other ways, and the added certitude that those industries have substantial, if immeasurable, external
economies combined to make the American scene a
potentially fertile ground for such analytical demon-
strations to flourish in a symbiotically interacting relationship between the theorists and the interest groups.
The focus on unfair trade became correspondingly
intensified.

These converging forces have resulted in a capture
and protectionist misuse of the traditional unfair trade
mechanisms in regard to *import* competition, CVD and
AD, in both the European Community and the United
States, as documented splendidly by Michael Finger,
Brian Hindley, and Patrick Messerlin in recent years;[4]
an extension of the unfair trade concerns to markets
for *exports*, in others' home markets and even in third
markets; and an expansion of such concerns to wholly
new areas (such as differences in retail distribution systems, savings rates, and workers' rights) in regard to
fair competition in both imports and exports. The last
two developments are more novel and merit further
comment.

The notion of unfair trade in one's export markets
has led not merely to conventional concerns about
subsidies to one's rivals there, but to two new twists.
First, the question of *intrasectoral reciprocity* of trade
barriers has become fairly widespread by now. Unfairness is in the eye of the one who makes the charge
and, if cars pay a 20 percent tariff in Sweden and none
in the United States, this is now considered unfair to
the United States, whereas only some "average" in-
equality (across all imports) of mutual openness of the
two countries would have sufficed to meet the crite-
rion earlier. The sensitivity has been accentuated, as I
argued earlier, by the theoretical possibility of large

19

adverse impact from such sectorwise nonreciprocity of barriers.

Second, the question of fairness is now considered important enough to justify actions that can only be described as reopening the terms of earlier trade negotiations in view of "ex post" realities. This is certainly one of the many arguments for seeking unrequited trade concessions from Japan: that the difficulty of penetrating her markets was underestimated and hence the trade concessions given to her were more than those received and the situation must be corrected by new concessions by Japan. An alternative variant of such "reopening" of the terms of the trade concessions is the notion that, given America's shift in comparative advantage to services, the earlier mutuality of openness with other countries is no longer valid, since services (unlike manufactures) are not subject to GATT discipline and have extensive NTBs. A new bargain incorporating services, and therefore reflecting better "average" reciprocity of openness, is thus necessary for the United States, failing which her trading partners will enjoy an unfair advantage.

These notions are dangerous enough and have driven some of the recent GATT-illegal aggressive unilateralism that I will discuss presently. But they are benign compared to the extension of unfair trade notions to wholly new areas, as in the 1988 Omnibus Trade and Competitiveness Act in the United States and in the Structural Impediments Initiative (SII) with Japan. In both instances, the notion of unreasonable, unfair trade practices has been extended to areas that range over matters as diverse as domestic antimonopoly policies, retail distribution systems, infrastructure spending, savings rates, workers' rights, and so on. The American shopping list in the SII talks was reputed to include 240 items!*

The problem with trying to include such things, and indeed all policies and institutions, as the natural target for objections that they affect trade and must therefore be scrutinized and changed to suit one's advantage if free trade is to be allowed, is simply that one is opening up a Pandora's box. Those who seek this wider mandate in looking for policy and institutional differences as sources of unfair trade are essentially arguing that everything affects trade, that policy (or absence thereof) on virtually everything will affect trade, and therefore that every policy can be put on the line in discussing what is "fair trade" and hence a prerequisite for legitimate free trade.

Thus, if Bangladesh has a current comparative advantage in textiles, due to lower wages, we no longer need to worry about being scolded as protectionists when we reject imports of Bangladeshi textiles as unfair trade caused by her "pauper labor." After all, the low Bangladeshi wages are a result of inadequate population control *policies* and of inefficient economic policies that inhibit investment and growth and hence a rise in real wages. In like manner, if the United States continues to produce textiles, which rely heav-

* The "true" objective behind SII, on the part of the U.S. administration, may have been to deflect the Japan-worriers and Japan-bashers away from concentration on trade and onto macroeconomic issues. But it inevitably became, in the Congress, a catalogue of unfair trade practices and Japanese trade barriers. The eventual Japanese accommodation of some demands, such as those for infrastructure spending, was also universally reported in the U.S. media as agreement to "open" Japanese markets even though it was primarily a political act to defuse the anti-Japanese sentiments.

ily on immigrant labor, often illegal, this is unfair trade, since American immigration *policy* encourages this outcome, and therefore a Structural Impediments Initiative demand for changed immigration policy needs to be made against the United States simply to ensure level playing fields.

In going down this unwise trade route, the American trade policymakers put the world trading system at risk: If *everything* becomes a question of fair trade, the likely outcome will be to diminish greatly the possibility of agreeing to a rules-oriented trading system. "Managed trade" will then be the outcome, with bureaucrats allocating trade according to what domestic lobbying pressures and foreign political muscle dictate.

CHAPTER THREE

The Issue of Managed Trade

THE QUESTION of managed trade has arisen as a threat to the fix-rule GATT regime, not just because of the outbreak of unfair-trademindedness. It has also derived from three other notions: (1) most trade is managed trade anyway. (2) Japan, a major player today, is exotic and different; she will not, and cannot, play by rules. (3) High-tech industries are so important that they cannot be, or will not be, left to the marketplace. Each contention is erroneous, though simplistic and superficially beguiling. Consider each in turn:

MANAGED TRADE ANYWAY?

That trade occurs frequently by either bypassing or flouting the GATT discipline, as with VERs on goods, or outside of its framework, as in agriculture and services, is indeed true. But it is a non sequitur to conclude that rules do not work and more managed trade must therefore be the way to go.[1] Yes, the glass is half empty and half full. But there is little doubt that it would have been emptier still if the GATT had not provided the overall framework and ethos that kept the glass upright instead of falling on its side. Moreover, the issue surely is whether we want to empty the glass further or to fill it up. The Uruguay Round is properly about filling it further.

THE JAPAN QUESTION

The "Japan question" raises different issues but, for recent critics, leads to a similar conclusion: that managed trade with Japan is either inevitable or desirable.

In particular, culturalists have had a field day with their assertion that Japan's cultural uniqueness makes fix-rule trade with her impossible to contemplate. Thus, James Fallows of *The Atlantic Monthly*, a journalist of great distinction and an influential Japan-worrier today, has argued that Japan is unable to play by principles, leading her to avoid rules under which the chips fall where they may. Instead, she prefers "quantities," making managed trade (with specified quantities traded) the only way to trade with her. Let Fallows speak for himself:

> Japanese society's lack of interest in principle has a profound effect that most Americans are slow to recognize. The lack of interest in principle makes sheer power the main test of what is "fair." . . .
>
> For example, when foreign competitors ask Japan to embrace the principles of free trade, they run up against not only Japan's special interests that would be hurt by imports but also a broader *Japanese discomfort with the very prospect of abiding by abstract principles*.
>
> A British friend gave this illustration, from the negotiations about seats for foreign firms on the Tokyo Stock Exchange: "Our position was that, in principle, any company that met the financial and other standards should be allowed to enter the market. Each time we said that, the Japanese reply was, 'How many seats do you want?' We would say, 'We don't know how many,

24

we want it to be open to any qualified applicant.' And they would say, 'Do you want two seats? Do you want three?'" The British negotiators eventually decided that two British companies seemed qualified, so they told the Japanese, "We want two." The Japanese side went back to deliberate—and in that time another qualified British firm appeared. My friend said, "They were incensed at us for not sticking to our word and not knowing what we wanted. I'm sure they thought it was a case of Western deception. The principle of free entry never had a chance." In the wrangle over beef and citrus imports Michael Smith, a blustery U.S. trade negotiator, got nowhere arguing that import quotas should, in principle, be relaxed. Then his side calculated that the beef quotas had a price effect equivalent to a 376 percent tariff—and he asked that the tariff be reduced, in stages, by 306 points. On the basis of this concrete demand, rather than any airy principle, a deal was struck.

Americans tend to squirm about the messiness of their two best-known trade agreements with Japan: the "voluntary limitations" that have restricted exports of Japanese cars to the United States since 1981, and the semiconductor agreement of 1986, which declared by fiat that foreign manufacturers should get 20 percent of semiconductor sales in Japan. These agreements are embarrassing to the United States because they so blatantly violate the principle of free competition; they assign market share by fiat, rather than leaving it to the free play of competitive forces. While the details of these agreements may displease the Japanese, they are perfectly comfortable with the basic concept. Like many of their own industrial understandings, it helps avoid "confusion" in the market.[2]

Fallows admits to no doubts here. Yet he must have noticed Japan's many children working their way up the educational ladder through competition that is as fair-minded, if excruciating, as anyone could desire. As one contrasts this with the substantially socially defined entrance to English public schools and their distant cousins in New England's best private schools, one wonders which society is characterized by greater fairness and adherence to principles.

Nor is Fallows on firmer ground on the Japanese inability to deal with rules-oriented trade. It is not convincing to assert that Japan's preference for quantities in dealing with us is entirely a reflection of Japan's exotic culture. It surely has *something* to do with the fact that we have insisted in our negotiations, and in the frenzy on Capitol Hill, on judging Japan's openness by how much we export. Faced with this unreasonable demand, the Japanese can fully be expected to say to themselves: How much must we import from the Americans to satisfy their unreasonable but persistent concerns and thus to get them off our backs? In short, the results orientation, as contrasted with a rules orientation, of their occasional questions to our negotiators can be as much a function of *our* political preferences today in trade with Japan as it is alleged to be a function of *their* cultural preferences.

In fact, history should suffice to inform us that the Japanese have handled their exports in this quantity-oriented fashion since the 1930s, when their diplomats were scurrying around the world, negotiating "voluntary export restraints" on their exports of textiles, pencils, and electric lamps to the United Kingdom, the United States, Australia, and other countries, many of whom enjoyed bilateral surpluses with Japan, *and* during years when Japan had overall multilateral deficits as well. Indeed, quite regardless of the balance of payments, the "Japan (trade) problem" has long been with us and has reflected Japan's rapid growth, her dependence on imports for raw materials, and her consequent rapid growth of exports, which has been hard to accommodate in the more sluggish world economy; the "giant among Lilliputians" (Bhagwati 1989a) has in consequence been repeatedly tied down by quantity restraints on her trade. If the Japanese negotiate on quantities (and tend to prefer settling trade disputes bilaterally instead of playing by multilateral rules, whose protection they should enjoy as well as provide to others), can it not be that they have learned from their trade history that this is the only way left open to them by their trading partners?*

Nor should one forget the irony that the large numbers of voluntary export restrictions that the United States has imposed on shoes, autos, etc., in recent years, setting quantitative limits on how much we will import of these items from Japan and other targeted nations, could equally be cited by a Japanese Fallows as a surefire proof of *American* distaste for abstract principles.

Again, the argument is often made that the Japanese behave differently in competition. They are "preda-

---

* Incidentally, the assertion that the Japanese are perfectly happy with the notion of import targets on semiconductors is surely inaccurate. Fallows also misconstrues the question of quotas and tariffs. Converting quotas into tariffs and then reducing them represents a popular strategy for import liberalization since quotas are doubly bad: They discriminate between sources, and they restrict. The general impression at the time was that it was the *Americans* who preferred beef quota enlargement instead because they were afraid that the shift to tariffs and then reductions therein would mean that the United States would lose to more efficient Australian suppliers.

tory," to use the description ascribed to Chalmers Johnson of the University of California at San Diego, and hence need to be restrained: Our rules are meaningless for such predators. I find this contention mildly amusing. The notion that American and other companies, by contrast, are "benign" competitors is quite silly. What the Cambridge economist Joan Robinson used to call the "animal spirits" of capital entrepreneurs surely are manifest in the United States and in Europe as much as in Japan: The jugular is certainly the preferred target of all, though the Japanese may be better at times in getting there. The successful always appear predatory. This was exactly the stereotype of British entrepreneurs during the nineteenth century, and of the "ugly Americans" in the 1950s, and 1960s. I like to remind the petulant critics of Japanese predation, and proclivity to unfair trade practices in pursuit of such predation, that a recent Davos Symposium survey of two thousand CEOs of corporations around the world that asked, "Who is the unfairest of them all?" found (as one would expect) the Japanese and then the South Koreans at the head of the list. But the third place of honor went to the United States, still a major presence in the world economy and successful beyond the fears that the diminished giant syndrome produces![3] Success certainly breeds resentment and envy, reinforcing fearful cultural stereotypes.

In fact, many of these cultural stereotypes are invoked much too readily to mark the Japanese as exotically different when, in fact, their differential behavior can be explained by differences of economic situation. One typical example is provided by the common notion that Japanese firms, unlike Western firms, believe in permanent employment because of the persistence of traditional familial values. But when this phenome-

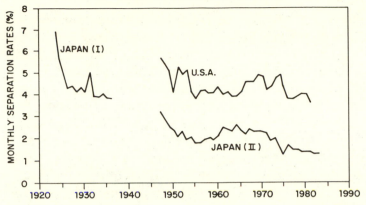

Figure 1. Historical Changes in Monthly Separation Rates in Manufacturing Industry in Japan and the United States: 1920s–1980s.
Source: Mincer and Higuchi 1988.

non is examined more closely, one finds that labor turnover, measured as monthly separation rates, in manufacturing industry in Japan before the Second World War was as high as in the postwar United States but dropped sharply *after* the war (see Figure 1). The "permanence" of employment is a recent development, which arose precisely when the familial values were coming under the pressures that increasing Westernization traditionally generates. Mincer and Higuchi (1989) have argued plausibly that the reduction in turnover can be explained instead by the rapid absorption of new technology in Japanese industry, with associated specificity of skills formation on the job that makes higher retention of the labor force economically profitable.

Another widely held belief about Japan's oddity, whose xenophobic consequences are assumed to require chastising and corrective response, relates to the discriminatory purchasing habits of Japanese foreign investors (who buy mostly from other Japanese).

Thus, for evidence, it is alleged that the ratio of imported components to value added is twice as much for Japanese investors in the United States as it is for others. But think again. If protection, or the threat of it, induces foreign firms to enter a market, they will typically import as many components as they can from their home base, where production is cheaper. Who can deny that the American resort to actual and threatened trade restraints against Japan has been substantially greater than against other OECD nations?* The astonishing thing may well be that Japanese investors have not wound up showing a yet higher ratio of imports to value added.

On the same issue, much has been made of Kreinin's (1988) recent study of the buying practices of sixty-two subsidiaries of Japanese, European, and American multinationals in Australia, which concludes that the Japanese sourced their supplies mostly from home while the others shopped around. But, aside from the question raised by the arbitrary selection of firms, Kreinin does not come to terms with the fact that sourcing of supplies from the home market is a common practice at the outset of a firm's coming into a market and that the Japanese manufacturing invest-

---

* Japanese direct investment in the United States was different from other OECD countries' investments in the first half of the 1980s, not merely in being induced by the conventional desire to "jump the tariff," since the threat of protection was directed more substantially at Japan. Much of it may have been prompted by the desire to *defuse* that threat instead by buying goodwill through job creation, etc. The protection-defusing direct investment, christened by me (Bhagwati 1986) as quid pro quo investment (since the firm invests in period 1, at a loss, to earn the quid pro quo of reduced protection in period 2), was uniquely Japanese in the early 1980s and has been extensively analyzed in recent theoretical literature by Dinopoulos (1989), Wong (1990), and others.

ment in Australia is of quite recent vintage. As Saxon-house (1991) has correctly noted,

[The Japanese manufacturing investment in Australia] is designed to produce substitutes for products which were until recently exported (and indeed continue to be exported) to Australia from Japan. Japan continues to retain (or until recently retained) a comparative advantage in most of what it is producing in Australia. Japanese manufacturing in Australia is an effort to put more value-added into the Australian economy, but Japanese ability to maintain and expand its market position there more likely rests on what it imports from home. By contrast, much of the European and American direct investments in Australia with which Kreinin compares Japanese practices were made a decade or more (in some instances six or seven decades) ago. While originally substitutes for exports, many of these investments are in product lines where the home country of the firm making the investment has long since lost much of its comparative advantage. It is hardly surprising that, unlike the Australian subsidiaries of Japanese firms, the Australian subsidiaries of European and American firms should have to source broadly in order to retain their local market share.

Kreinin's findings for Australia are entirely consistent with the traditional histories of multinational corporations and overseas direct investment and do not suggest truly distinctive Japanese practices. The early history of Ford and GM, among other American enterprises in Japan, is hardly different from the Japanese experience.

Then again, the Japanese firms are known to develop longer-term supplier relationships, using subcontracting to fewer suppliers and greater monitoring of these suppliers' design and quality. But, as John McMillan, a distinguished economist pioneering the study of the optimal design of incentives, has observed, little of this has to do with "Japanese consensus culture" or with coziness in personal relationships and cultural bias in favor of dealing with those in one's social group. Rather, longer-term relationships make substantial economic sense, just as marriage is preferable to promiscuity by other criteria. McMillan's (1989) careful study of U.S. and Japanese industry concludes, in fact, that "the relationship between procuring firms and supplying firms in the United States seems to be moving towards [the more efficient] Japanese methods of production. . . . Japanese industry can be understood as having attained, at the end-point of an evolutionary process, a complex system of incentives, to which firms respond rationally."

We must then reject the cultural stereotypes that lead many to conclude that Japan is abnormal and bizarre to the point where rules-oriented trade, with mutual advantage, is not possible with her. The alleged differences are often illusory or exaggerated. Or they can be explained for the most part by the differential constraints and circumstances that lead to different outcomes from similar "economizing" behavior. There is much less here than meets the eye as the culturalists scan the Japanese landscape, start climbing up the wall and urge us to join them in the call for managed trade with Japan.

Economists are generally immune to such seduction. But not always: Some have fallen prey. The ladder that these few economists have climbed to get on board with the culturalists in their assertion of Japan's uniqueness and inability to play by the rules under a

GATT-type system is naturally different. It has taken the form that Japan's imports are "too few" by the standards of the rest of us, that this is proof of Japan's cheating to flout the rules or her exotic economic organization that makes the rules infructuous, and that therefore only managed trade can enable us to export to Japan effectively and fairly (reciprocating our own imports from them).[4] A favorite proposal is to give the Japanese definite targets for imports and whip them with retributive tariffs if they fail to fulfill them[5]—a proposal that fails the elementary tests of common sense and economic soundness in ignoring the fact that targets with deadlines are meaningful only for centrally planned economies. Targets are also silly and dangerous (because they are not necessarily within the government's policy reach) in countries with large private sectors. Besides, retributive tariffs would be GATT-illegal, an issue to which I return later.

Now, it is interesting to observe that the recent critical focus on Japan's imports, and their inadequacy, parallels the long-standing aversion to Japan's exports, and their abundance. To be sure, the notion that Japan cannot be accommodated within a rules-oriented world trading system is nothing new. What is novel, rather, is the extension of this view, hitherto confined to Japan's exports, to Japan's imports. As I remarked earlier, the Japanese diplomats have been busy since the 1930s, negotiating restraints on their exports in a world that found these exports politically hard to accept and legitimated these restraints by conveniently hiding behind the view of Japan as an unfair trader.

In fact, informed scholars of international trade know that the fear of Japan, and the stereotypes of its unfair trade practices, were so commonplace that when the GATT was formed, the vanquished Germany was admitted to it but Japan was kept out for almost a decade (see the splendid account of Japan's myriad problems in becoming a GATT member in Gardner Patterson (1966, ch. 6), who correctly concludes that discrimination *against* Japan has been considerable and has been motivated by protectionist objectives). Japan would not become a contracting party to the GATT until September 1955. Even then, fourteen countries, representing 40 percent of GATT membership and also of Japan's exports to the GATT members then, invoked Article XXXV, under which they need not undertake GATT-defined obligations to the new member: an action that was GATT-legal but unprecedented in GATT's short life.[6] For years thereafter, Japan would be negotiating for its full GATT rights with these countries.

Through these postwar years of blatant anti-Japanese trade discrimination, the United States was enlightened. Its efforts to get Japan into the GATT were persistent and unrelenting. Narrow American economic interest was also congruent with this enlightened policy. Given the commitment to rebuild Japan, less trade meant more American aid. Also, trade discrimination by others meant more spillover Japanese exports to the United States, making the politics of trade liberalization more difficult. American economic strength after the war also made the enlightened policy toward Japan more palatable: The fear of Japan was absent, whereas in war-devastated Europe it was palpable.

The good sense on Japan has eroded as the Japan-fixated culturalists and economists have rekindled the old fears of Japan, reviving stereotypes that had mostly disappeared from view.* This motley crew is now described in the media, and indeed see themselves, as "revisionists," who are engaged in the task of rescuing the rest of us from the complacency arising from "conventional wisdom," which is the polite phrase for the folly afflicting lazy minds. In fact, in the historical perspective I have just sketched, they are nothing of the kind. In returning us to the old and fearful stereotypes, these "revisionists" are actually regressionists, whose prejudicial "findings" against Japan should produce only a sense of *deja vu* and despair among us.

Nonetheless, the questions have been raised and have preoccupied economists: *Are* Japan's imports too low and, if so, what does this signify? On the first question, it is perhaps not entirely a coincidence that the regressionists on Japan among the economists are also simple-minded regressionists who rely on such arguments as "Well, the ratio of manufactured imports to GNP has remained unchanged at 2% for years." But against these double-regressionists, we can turn to sophisticated econometric analyses by a number of more serious and scholarly analysts. These analyses show that the evidence of Japan's under-

---

* Perhaps the stereotypes were captured most elegantly by Ogden Nash (1940):

> How courteous is the Japanese;
> He always says, "Excuse it, please."
> He climbs into his neighbor's garden,
> And smiles, and says, "I beg your pardon."
> He bows and grins a friendly grin,
> And calls his hungry family in;
> He grins and bows a friendly bow;
> "So sorry, this my garden now."

achievement in terms of imports is much more ambiguous. In fact, the recent work of Gary Saxonhouse and of Ed Leamer, both working with well-specified trade models, shows that Japan's total imports and imports of manufactures are well within the margin of what one would expect, given her lack of natural resources, resource endowments, etc. This is the conclusion of a careful, technical review of several econometric studies of Japan's imports-to-GNP performance by Srinivasan and Hamada (1989). These authors conclude that the studies of Saxonhouse (1983, 1988) and Leamer (1988) are the best crafted and that "the empirical support in favor or against the hypothesis that Japanese are underimporting is subject to criticisms which are most damaging particularly to studies in favor of the hypothesis." The contention that intra-industry imports of manufactures are too low is also subject to the problems that to a critical degree, these measures of intraindustry trade are artifacts of statistical aggregation because the analyst uses international trade statistics that group all kinds of goods into one "industry" and the conceptual basis of such estimates is pretty murky, in consequence.[7]

One needs instead micro-level studies of mutual trade among countries for meaningfully defined industries, but these are scarce. If they were abundant, one might find in specific cases of "low" imports but "high" exports by Japan that there were perfectly good and harmless reasons for such an outcome (just as the reverse phenomenon could be found in specific industries for any other country or pair of countries and then explained in similar, innocuous ways). Thus, for instance, differences in Japan's tastes, interpreted broadly, could account for low imports of specific big-ticket items: There may have been low demand in

Japan for the large gas guzzlers the United States specialized in until recently, while the Japanese specialization in small cars had a segment of the more diversified market abroad; or large refrigerators could not be used in Japan's small apartments. Careful micro-level studies would get at such phenomena, where they arise, and provide more natural and less adversarial explanations for their occurrence. They would also lay to rest the wild assertions about Japan's closed markets that surface from time to time, are found credible in the current hysterical climate, and are often seen on examination to be fictional. Thus, the U.S. trade representative, Ambassador Carla Hills, on one of her negotiating visits to Tokyo, was reported to have relied on her advisers to assert that foreign baby bottles could not make it to Tokyo, only to be disabused by her Japanese hosts, who immediately produced the evidence of their availability in the stores. Again, on being assured by a Japan-worrier that Kodak film was not available in Tokyo's retail outlets ("while Fuji was in New York's"), she was surprised to find on investigation of the matter that this was not true.

The case that Japan's imports, whether total or of manufactures, are abnormally low, when set against predictions by international trade economists of what they should be, is thus seriously weak, and the best-crafted research militates against it.* But even if the

---

* I should add that economists recently have started looking also at price statistics to see if they can infer Japan's elusive closedness by showing that prices in Japan are higher than what they would be if the market were open. But little damaging evidence has arisen from this approach either: First, the examination of overall price levels, which are readily available and were used for this purpose, tells one little about the question of closedness, for the overall price level includes prices of nontraded goods, much

findings had gone the other way, it would not follow that the explanation of Japan's underimporting was necessarily to be found in Japan or that rules-oriented trade with it was impossible.

Over the long haul, by and large, the demonstration that Japan was importing too little would imply

---

the most important part of the economy, and these can go in different directions that do not have a unique relationship to closedness of markets. Just as Japan's price level is too high at prevailing exchange rates, it was too low in the 1950s, for instance; and just as the latter was not a sign of Japan's openness, the former is not a sign of her closedness. Second, price data have been collected now only for traded goods, in another attempt to correct them for quality and other differences (such as whether the price quotations are from discount houses or department stores). Collected jointly by the U.S. Department of Commerce and the Japanese MITI, these data are for items that were not selected randomly but were instead chosen after endless wrangling between the two agencies: A scientist would tend to reject the data out of hand, in consequence; but the data are nonetheless of interest, as they provide some information in place of the usual assertions. And that information is revealing. It turned out that there was little evidence of the Japanese producers' prices being cheaper in the United States than in Japan: Of fourteen Japanese-produced cameras and video camera–related products, only six were cheaper in the United States. And, altogether, only twenty-six of fifty-seven Japanese products were found to be cheaper the United States than in Japan. By contrast, only four out of thirty-five U.S. products and only two out of twenty-one European products were cheaper in Japan than in the United States (Saxonhouse 1990; Cline 1990). While one can think of *ad hoc* reasons for this asymmetry, it is surely odd that it exists. It suggests, as Cline (1990) notes, that the problem is one of high-quality foreign producers undertaking oligopolistic pricing at the high-price end of the Japanese market, operating on the low-volume, high-price strategy. This strategy does mean, for these products, that arbitrage is not eliminating the high price in Japan; but that could be due to a host of factors, such as scale economies in transportation, ability to differentiate the product for Japanese consumers (e.g., left-hand drive specially made for the Japanese auto market while U.S. cars are right-hand drives), etc.

equally that Japan was exporting too little. The cause of the low import share could then equally be protection *against* Japan. Since the European Community has been effectively using AD mechanisms to erect Fortress Europe against Japan for over a decade, and the United States has also used VERs and other restrictions against important Japanese exports, the paradox I am noting is not a theoretical curiosity. It certainly goes to the heart of the matter at hand.

Again, even if the Japanese market is open and can be penetrated, the *perception* or belief that it is not may prevent attempts at penetration, or lead to hasty withdrawal after short penetration, by the foreign exporters.

An apt analogy is provided by the phenomenon of international migration. It is common knowledge among scholars that the mere presence of a high-wage country is not sufficient to generate economic immigration from a low-wage economy: It is only a necessary condition for such immigration. It is only if a rivulet of immigration is somehow opened up that the flow takes on greater dimensions. Thus, for instance, there was negligible immigration from Mexico across the Rio Grande into the United States until the twentieth century. Chinese and Japanese immigration was the order of the day until the passage of the Oriental Exclusion acts in California at the beginning of this century prompted American recruiters to go south and begin getting Mexicans for farming and other work. This opened up Mexican immigration, which then swelled to the substantial levels that dominate the current discussions of U.S. immigration dilemmas and policy.

The perception that Japan is not open, or that even if it is open (that is, not subject to significant tariffs and nontariff barriers imposed by the government), it is nearly impossible to penetrate, is certainly a phenomenon that could be explained by long-standing experience with the history of Japan's policy of "controlled openness," which gave foreigners heavily circumscribed access to Japan and simultaneously prevented the colonization that brought many other non-Western cultures and economies closer to Western norms in modern times. Commodore Perry's "black ships" arrived in 1853 in Japan, and the first full commercial treaty was signed with the United States in 1858; with similar treaties to follow with the European powers, "treaty ports" were opened, including Nagasaki, Kanagawa, and principally Yokohama, to foreign residence and trade; and the residences of foreigners elsewhere were confined to areas set aside as Foreign Settlements.[8]

The postwar reconstruction of Japan meant more Westernization of Japan under the Occupation. It also was under a protectionist umbrella, as much as Europe's was during the long period of current-account exchange restrictions. The net effect was therefore to maintain the perception of Japan as closed to imports right into the 1970s. By the early 1980s, however, the protectionist barriers were down, as elsewhere, and Japan's markets were open, but the perceptions of closedness persisted and would spill over into massive complaints, bordering on paranoia and petulance, from time to time.

If this thesis is correct, then a dramatic change would shift this perception sufficiently to generate a distinct surge in Japanese imports of manufactures. This, in fact, appears to have happened with the big change in the yen's value after the Plaza Agreement. The rapid and substantial rise in the value of the yen increased imports in two ways: through the cheapening of imports (which is the conventional effect) and by eroding therewith the self-fulfilling pessimism about entering the Japanese market (which is the novel "perception problem" effect I have just sketched).

When the behavior of Japanese imports of manufactures in the latter half of the 1980s is examined, one is in for a surprise if one has been feeding on a steady diet of allegations of Japan's closedness. A few key facts are sufficient. Figure 2 shows Japan's substantial rate of increase (in value) of manufactured imports from different sources during 1986–1989, while Figure 3 shows that, at an annual average, the 1985–1988 import growth performance of Japan exceeded that of

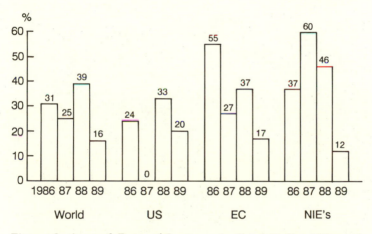

Figure 2. Annual Rate of Increase in Total Dollar Value of Japan's Manufactured Imports from Different Sources: 1986–1989.

Source: Japan Ministry of International Trade and Industry (MITI); based on customs clearance statistics.

Note: NIEs are the Newly Industrialized Economies.

41

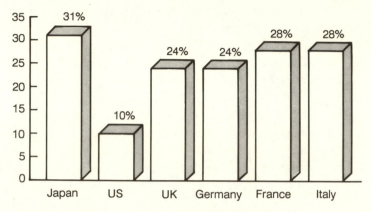

Figure 3. Average Annual Rate of Increase in Total Dollar Value of Manufactured Imports: 1985–1988.

Source: MITI.

Note: The U.S. growth rate was 20 percent during 1982–1985, when the dollar was overvalued.

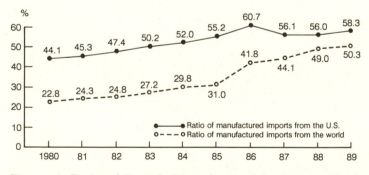

Figure 4. Ratio of Japan's Manufactured Imports to Total Imports.

Source: MITI; based on customs clearance statistics.

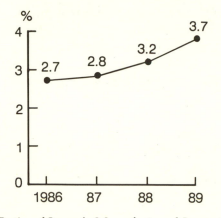

Figure 5. Ratio of Japan's Manufactured Imports to GNP. *Source*: MITI.

several major OECD countries, and was over three times that of the United States. Again, in contrast to the presumption that manufactured imports are an unduly low and stagnant proportion of Japan's total imports, the statistics show (see Figure 4) that the ratio of Japan's manufactured to total imports has grown steadily, rising from 22.8 percent in 1980 to 50.3 percent in 1989, while the same ratio for imports only from the United States has also increased between these years, from 44.1 percent to 58.3 percent. As for the ratio of Japan's manufactured imports to GNP, this alleged "eternal constant" (Dornbusch 1989) has gone from 2.7 percent in 1986 to 3.7 percent in 1989 (see Figure 5). Moreover, this has happened while little has been done by Japan to "open" her markets, underlining my view that the "problem" has been on the supply side of the equation (which *has* changed dramatically, in the ways I have outlined).

43

The proposition (dearly loved by exporting interests who would profit from getting privileged access to Japan's lucrative market, by culturalists who are victims of discredited stereotypes, and by economists who should know better) that managed trade with Japan in the form of quantity targets of voluntary import expansion (VIEs) must be the only way to trade with Japan is therefore wholly unconvincing. It must be rejected firmly.

HIGH-TECH INDUSTRIES

The Japan question feeds an altogether different argument in the United States for managed trade, however, that is more universal. This relates to the fear (which I discussed earlier) that unless trade restrictions and targets are imposed on high-tech industries, these industries will be lost to countries such as Japan, which somehow manage to spawn and support them against the firms in countries that abstain from such support.

Now, while economists have great difficulty in finding externalities in specific industries and are generally inclined to discount claims of their existence in a sufficiently disproportionate degree to justify selective support, the opposite is true of politicians. Today, thanks to the scientific revolution that started in informatics and biogenetics, there is virtually no politician in any major OECD country who does not feel that high-tech industries must be attracted and supported for their manifest externalities and, in noneconomic terms, for their identification with modernization in view of their state-of-the-art, at-the-frontier status.

Given these perceptions, which then become realities that the economists must work with, it is evident
that a rules-oriented free trade system in high-tech industries will not be workable unless *either* there is a
multilateral mechanism for bringing up front the vari-
ous differing ways in which different governments are
alleged to be biasing the outcomes in their favor, so
that the "net balance" of such artificial advantages
among the different rivals is sorted out and then eliminated, *or* one goes yet further and manages essentially to get an acceptable degree of harmonization
(that then irons out the differences) by adherence to a
code of do's and don'ts. The latter may not be possible
if governments do have distinct preferences for certain policies; the former surely is possible and would
enable the Japanese to point to the artificial advantages stemming in the United States from higher defense expenditures, support for science through the
National Science Foundation, etc., when the Americans complain about the Japanese government's guidance and support to pooled research, etc. The multilateral format would ensure that the finger-pointing
would be fair and balanced, where appropriate, without the advantage of the thicker finger in bilateral one-
on-one confrontations.

This solution where the trade issue would be managed by institutional innovation so as to maintain the
fix-rule regime in high-tech industries was proposed
by me some three years ago:

> [A]n international consensus on the desirability of
> achieving a *broad* intra-sectoral balance of artificial ad-
> vantages in a *narrow* range of such industries would be
> a useful supplement to the world trade regime. The
> emphasis, however, should not be on bilateral negotia-

tions (in which the strong countries would browbeat the weak); it should be on multilateral procedures for determining fairly the broad balance of artificial supports in different countries in the industry in question.[9]

The idea of an official code for high-tech has now been taken up also by Sylvia Ostry in a 1990 study of trade and innovation policies in the triad constituted by the United States, Europe, and Japan:

> The objectives of the [OECD] initiative would be to do the following:
>
> • Review the theoretical and empirical literature on "strategic industries" with a view to proposing a *consensus working definition* for policy use.
>
> • Analyze the three elements of the policy set— trade, R&D, and market structure policies—in (initially) the Triad, with a view to highlighting the *impact* of significant differences in policy *on industrial and trade performance.*
>
> • Make recommendations for *short-run* action (to defuse international friction) and to implement a *longer-run process of policy convergence.*[10]

It is important to emphasize, however, that these proposals are for "trade management," *not* for "managed trade." A fix-rule regime is consistent with the former; in fact, Tokyo Round codes, negotiations of trade barrier reductions, establishment of new disciplines, enforcement of one's trade rights, and assurance of observation of one's trade obligations are all part of "trade management."

"Managed trade," on the other hand, is the antithesis of the fix-rule regime. I emphasize this simply because, with the free entry of amateurs into this politically rewarding field, the two wholly opposed concepts are increasingly confused and used interchangeably, crying out for a George Orwell to set things right. [The distinction between "trade management" and "managed trade" and other conceptual matters are discussed fully in Appendix I.]

Would what I have proposed really work? It would not if the result of fix-rule trade in high-tech were to leave Japan, the United States, or the European Community without high-tech, that is, in jargon, if we were to get corner solutions. But surely that is utterly improbable. All three areas have high skills, research and development capacities, capital formation, and access to foreign capital and know-how in a highly interdependent world economy. Is it really credible that open markets would take high-tech wholly, or substantially, out of any of these areas?

CHAPTER FOUR

Aggressive Unilateralism

THE CONCERNS over unfair trade have created yet another hazard for the fix-rule GATT system, cutting at the heart of multilateralism, in the recent use of aggressive unilateralism by the United States to impose on others its unilaterally defined views of unfair trade practices.

I refer here, of course, to the use of the Section 301 and "Super 301" provisions of the American trade legislation, as currently updated in the 1988 Act, to demand negotiations from specified countries on "priority" practices that the United States finds unacceptable, regardless of whether they are proscribed by GATT or another treaty, and to seek their abolition on a tight time schedule set by the United States, using tariff retaliation by the United States if necessary.[1] Japan, India, and Brazil were the three nations named in the Super 301 process on May 25, 1989; in 1990, Japan (which negotiated its way out) and Brazil (which, with the change of presidents, shifted to a far more open trade policy than demanded under Super 301) were not named again, while India continued on the list.

In assessing this practice of aggressive unilateralism, and defining the nature of the threat it poses to multilateralism, it is useful to begin by noting that the conventional theory of trade allows for three types of trade concessions: unilateral concessions by oneself; mutual, reciprocal concessions; and unilateral concessions by others.

SUBSIDIESSSSS

KAL ©1990 Cartoonists & Writers Syndicate

Carla Hills, the U.S. trade representative, is credited with the metaphor of using a crowbar to pry open foreign markets, applying the policy of aggressive unilateralism embodied in recent U.S. trade legislation on Section 301 and Super 301 actions. While she has skillfully minimized the damage that such policy inflicts on the GATT-focused multilateral system, her image of a tough trade negotiator has grown out of recent Super 301 actions. This image is reflected in this cartoon, which appeared in *The Economist* at the time of the Houston Summit in July 1990, showing her wielding the crowbar as a batter in a baseball game, with European farm subsidies as the targeted ball.

UNILATERALISM FOR ONESELF

Unilateralism in trade liberalization by oneself is a dominant theme both in one variety of free trade doctrine and in the nineteenth-century British practice. Since the days of Adam Smith,[2] international economists have been aware that this presupposes the exogeneity of the foreigners' trading offer to one's policy: Else, as I remarked earlier, one could strategically use tariff (and other) policy to gain yet more from international trade. The issue was discussed at length by Marshall, Edgeworth, and other economists of the time when the British, faced by the rising competition from the United States and Germany, began debating the wisdom of their unilateral free trade in the face of the protection of these emergent economic powers. They opted for unilateralism on many diverse grounds, among them recent political economy–related worries about the capture by protectionists of retaliatory tariffs for their own use, indulgence towards others' infant industry tariffs, the British lack of sufficient economic power, etc.[3] The exogeneity of others' trade offers to one's tariff policy was therefore a policy assumption that came largely from the assumed lack of power or from refusal to indulge the power either because of the fear of outweighing harm from side effects (through misuse) or from the perception that others' (infant industry) tariffs were economically justified and hence contributed to world efficiency even if they harmed oneself.[4]

FIRST-DIFFERENCE RECIPROCITY

But unilateral trade liberalization for oneself did not find a place in the design of the GATT, which reflected instead the principle of "first-difference" reciprocity. While this approach is considered "mercantilist" by those who prefer unilateral trade liberalization by oneself, the pairing of mutual concessions has a fourfold advantage:

(1) If I can get you also to liberalize while I liberalize myself, I gain twice over;

(2) If there are "second-best" macroeconomic considerations, such as short-run balance of payments difficulties from trade liberalization, the mutuality of liberalization should generally diminish them;

(3) Mutuality of concessions suggests fairness and makes adjustment to trade liberalization politically more acceptable by the domestic losers from the change; and

(4) Foreign concessions to one's exporters create new interests that can counterbalance the interests that oppose one's own trade liberalization.

In short, the mutuality of concessions on a reciprocal basis offers some definite, practical advantages even though it builds on the notion, not consonant with good economic sense, that trade liberalization is a cost rather than a source of gain. In any event, (voluntary) unilateral embrace of free trade is generally about as palatable to countries—Hong Kong being one dramatic exception today—as is unilateral disarmament.

UNILATERALISM FOR OTHERS

What we have witnessed currently (from many proponents of Section 301 under the 1988 Trade Act of the United States), however, is the intention to extract unilateral, that is, unrequited, trade concessions from others. Why?

Theoretically, one can think of two sets of reasons why this policy may have been adopted by the United States: One malign and the other benign. Both sets serve the United States's interest and may therefore be described as national welfare reasons.

The malign national welfare reason is straightforward and, in fact, is one that every informed scholar of the theory of commercial policy teaches in the classroom. As long as trade is voluntary and left to market forces, we know that it will be a non-zero-sum game: It will benefit each party to the transaction. But while each gains from trade, we also teach that power can be used to extract greater gains from trade from the other party. Typically, the examples adduced are those of Nazi Germany and Stalin's Soviet Union, not that of the U.S. Congress using American muscle to extract concessions from weaker partners.

The use of power can, however, be argued very quickly to show that power may be used to force another country into making unilateral trade concessions and hence improving one's welfare. In jargon, the economist would say that power is used to improve one's terms of trade by reducing others' use of trade restrictions.

Needless to say, the malign use of economic power to force unilateral concessions from others would be welfare improving if these concessions were indeed so extracted. Recall that when the British debate at the end of the nineteenth century turned to examine this argument in the context of unilateral embrace of free trade, one of the main objections was that no such power existed in British trade. The willingness to resort to tariff retaliation, contrary to GATT obligations, and the size of the stake in the American market for the targets of such a tactic, have changed this presumption for today's United States, however.* That this malign, self-serving rationale motivates some to embrace Section 301's use of aggressive tactics to extract unilateral concessions from weaker trading partners is not in doubt. Again, the concessions made by countries such as South Korea to avoid Super 301 action on May 25, 1989, should have produced more converts in the U.S. Congress to the cynical view that this is Section 301's principal merit.

But fairness requires one to recognize that, while aggressive unilateralism may reflect the naked use of power to extract trading gains from weaker powers, this is not the full story. In fact, a close examination of the congressional debate and political pronouncements suggests strongly that the demands for unilateral concessions by others are often considered, in truth, to be not so. The mutuality of concessions is thought to be preserved by this generally fair-minded nation, despite the demands for apparently unrequited concessions, in a number of ways.

Elsewhere, I have considered several such "benign" rationales, concluding that most will not survive scrutiny.[5] Many are Japan focused: for instance, that Japan has nullified and impaired the fair value of its concessions by cheating and hence unilateral concessions from her are necessary to restore the mutuality under earlier Rounds of negotiated concessions; or that the

---

* It is therefore puzzling to see Paul Krugman (1990, 107) arguing that no such power exists: "We cannot expect to bully Europe or Japan into doing things our way any more than they could do the same to us." As scholars of Section 301 know well, and as I explain below, the problem with Section 301 arises precisely because the United States has the power to bully Japan, South Korea, etc., and has used it for getting trade concessions and the issue is whether this use of power is desirable or not!

difficulty of penetrating the Japanese market was underestimated and hence the mutual concessions, while balanced *ex ante*, have been unbalanced *ex post*, and Japan must make up for its undue gain by making unilateral concessions currently. Some arguments are more generic: for instance, that the successful developing countries, such as South Korea and Taiwan, must renounce Special and Differential treatment and assume new obligations to give market access (as part of their "graduation" to developed status) just as other developed countries do at the GATT.

In any event, the extraction of concessions from others by the use of threats of tariff retaliation, under time schedules set by the United States itself, represents a dramatic shift to a policy of aggressive unilateralism by a country whose leadership was central to the creation and maintenance of the GATT-centered multilateral trading system. Precisely how does this policy threaten this trading system?

At the outset, it must be understood that the GATT does have the force of a treaty for the United States. This was demonstrated by Jackson (1967) in a brilliant article, which is unfortunately not public knowledge in policy circles.

Now, when the United States retaliates, as it has already in some Section 301 actions, with its typical 100 percent *ad valorem* tariff applied selectively to the goods of the targeted country, the GATT-illegality is at several levels. The discriminatory nature of such tariffs violates Article I, which imposes the MFN obligation. Also, since the tariff is in practice likely to be bound at a lower level, the 100 percent punitive tariff will generally be in violation of Article II as well.

Why does GATT-illegality matter? *Prima facie*, honoring a treaty commitment is to reaffirm one's respect for orderly procedures and the rule of law in dealing with other nation-states.

But does vigilantism have a place when the sheriff is asleep in the saloon? Or, to rise to a higher principle, is there not a case of "justified disobedience," as Professor Robert Hudec has recently put it, when the law is not working as it should?[6] In either case, a doctrine of "creative illegality" is being invoked: A breach of law to improve the law is being claimed.

The problem with this line of defense by the United States of GATT-illegality (to improve an ineffective GATT) is that almost no one else in the trading system quite accepts this justification. Indeed, as Professor Hudec has noted, the United States's own record of acting within the rules to respect others' GATT-defined rights has not been exemplary.

There is also the problem that means may affect ends. Is it not likely that a declared willingness to break GATT commitments, and even actual breach thereof, may spread cynicism towards such commitments by others rather than adherence to them in the future?

Let me turn to other dangers inherent in this form of unilateral extraction of trade concessions from others. In particular, since it reflects clout and concentrated pressure, there is a strong likelihood that the targets of Section 301 actions will satisfy American demands by diverting trade from other countries (with small political clout) to the United States, satisfying the strong at the expense of the weak.

Admittedly, Ambassador Carla Hills, the U.S. trade representative, repeatedly stresses that she will ensure that markets are opened under Section 301 in a non-discriminatory fashion. But *ex ante* intentions can diverge from *ex post* outcomes. The lobbies in the United

States that drive USTR do not really care whether markets open generally: Their objective evidently is to increase their own exports. Equally, the countries targeted for action know that the American pressures are more likely to ease if the United States gets a good share than if it does not. The game is set up therefore in terms of implicit pro–trade diversion bias rules that all parties recognize as political realities.

There is also the possibility that the use of muscle to impose one's views and to extract one-way trade concessions will poison the ethos of fairness in trade relations, without which open markets are hard to sustain.

Even if one makes the implausible assumption that Section 301 will be used only for "altruistic" reasons (such as using muscle to make progress in the Uruguay Round negotiations),[7] the notion that the United States should serve as a benign dictator, laying down its own definition of a desirable trading regime instead of making (admittedly slower) progress by persuasion and mutual concession, is hard to accept. Institutions cannot be built on notions of benign dictatorship; this is a lesson that the functioning democracy in the United States itself, with all the slowness and "inefficiencies" that practitioners of realpolitik complain about, amply teaches us all.

We must also confront the fact that trade policy is rarely made in pluralistic democracies by dictators with monolithic objective functions. Instead, it reflects the resolution of sectional interests in the political domain. There is no necessary correspondence, therefore, between the triumphant sectoral interest and the national interest and, most important, the international or cosmopolitan interest that must define the world trading regime.[8]

The instrument of aggressive unilateralism there-fore has important drawbacks, and somehow we will have to find a way of cutting it down to size through an agreement proscribing the use of such instruments.

CHAPTER FIVE

Regionalism

THE QUESTION of regionalism has emerged recently with the moves to Europe 1992 and the U.S.-Canada Free Trade Agreement. These regional alignments have led to fears of fragmentation of the world economy into trading blocs in antithesis to GATT-wide multilateral free trade. Does such regionalism truly constitute a threat to multilateralism? If so, what is the nature of the threat? And what can be done to counter that threat?

AUTHORIZATION UNDER ARTICLE XXIV

Before these questions can be answered, it is necessary to recall that the GATT itself extends MFN only to its members and hence falls short of worldwide multilateralism. But the important point to remember is that it is open to membership to all who meet the criteria for admission and has generally been inclusive rather than exclusive.[1]

More important, however, from the viewpoint of regionalism is that Article XXIV of the GATT sanctions free trade areas and customs unions (which also have common external tariffs) and that the European Community and the U.S.-Canada Free Trade Agreement were consummated within Article XXIV itself. Thus, these regional blocs are indeed GATT-consistent, even if they may be considered threatening to GATT's basic conception of the world trading system.

THEORY OF PREFERENTIAL REDUCTIONS
OF TRADE BARRIERS

Then again, economic theory certainly does *not* come down wholly against preferential reductions of trade barriers, by any group of countries, such as a subset of the GATT members, whether that preferential reduction is 100 percent (as envisaged under Article XXIV) or less. To see this, consider first the theory of preferential reductions of trade barriers (or what international economists call, simply if somewhat inaccurately, the economic theory of customs unions). Today, this theory consists of four related, yet distinct, sets of analytical approaches.

Viner-Lipsey-Meade Approach

Jacob Viner (1950) introduced the seminal distinction between trade-creating and trade-diverting unions among a subset of countries that retained their respective external tariffs. The trade-creating union would create trade among the member countries at the expense of inefficient industries in the member countries. The trade-diverting union would do so at the expense of more efficient industries in nonmember countries.

Viner's main contribution was therefore to destroy the common fallacy that a preferential move toward (total) free trade was necessarily welfare improving and thus to demonstrate that all preferential paths to (total) free trade were not monotonic in welfare. From our current perspective, however, it can be read equally as saying that preferential moves can indeed be welfare improving: It just depends on the parameters.

But two further points, relevant to Article XXIV, also must be made. First, it is not necessary that preferential trade liberalization be 100 percent, as with a free trade area or customs union, for it to be welfare improving. Cuts of less than 100 percent in trade barriers, for instance, within a regional grouping, could be welfare improving. Second, James Meade's (1955) analysis showed that as tariffs were progressively cut within a union toward zero (that is, toward 100 percent liberalization), the gain from trade creation was less, while the probability of loss from trade diversion increased. Thus, a rule allowing 100 percent preferential liberalization, but not less, was perverse according to this line of analysis. Hence, Article XXIV, which insisted on 100 percent trade liberalization as a precondition for preferential groupings, both was too strict and, if anything, favored arrangements that were less likely to prove welfare improving than those that were proscribed.

Kemp-Wan Approach

An alternative theoretical approach, of considerable power and ingenuity, has been proposed by Murray Kemp and Henry Wan (1976), drawing inspiration from an earlier effort of Ohyama. It shows that any group of countries could always form a customs union, with a common external tariff, that had two desired properties: (1) The nonmembers would have their welfare unchanged; and (2) the members would improve their own welfare.

Theoretically, this is an important contribution because it shows that preferential groupings can always be devised, in principle, for any given subset of countries, such that they are a Pareto-improvement over the initial preunion situation. Pareto-improvement means that no country within the union is worse off and at least one is better off.[2] The question then, for policy, is whether the specific grouping proposed satisfies the sufficiency conditions for such Pareto-superior welfare-improving unions. But this is a question that is hard to answer since Kemp and Wan merely provide proof of the theoretical existence of such unions but do not provide any guidance as to the necessary and sufficient conditions that such unions must satisfy.

Cooper-Massell-Bhagwati Approach

Yet another approach to customs union theorizing, reflective of the concerns of small developing countries, was taken by Cooper and Massell (1965a, 1965b) and Bhagwati (1968) during the 1960s. They argued that, if a given target level of aggregate import-competing industrialization were the objective, the cost of it to developing countries with small markets could be reduced by unions that permitted trade and mutual exchange of industrial production among themselves (with scale economies exploited within the union) while maintaining protection against the manufacturers of the developed countries.

This argument builds on economies of scale but does not need to: Specialization in manufactures within the union would be profitable even without invoking scale economies. While it also treats any given degree of overall industrialization as a "noneconomic" objective, it has the flavor of the Kemp-Wan logic: The proposed union achieves gains for member countries subject to given import substitution for the aggregate union vis-à-vis the nonmember (developed) countries, which therefore leaves nonmember countries' welfare unchanged.

Brecher-Bhagwati Approach

The previous approaches consider either the welfare effects of forming arbitrarily specified customs unions (the Viner-Lipsey-Meade view) or the judicious formation of customs unions so as to achieve Pareto-better outcomes (the Kemp-Wan and Cooper-Massell-Bhagwati approaches). An alternative approach introduced by Brecher and Bhagwati (1981) provides instead the mechanism to analyze the welfare effects of parametric and policy variations in customs unions with common external tariffs and with freedom of intraunion factor movements.

In analyzing the effects of changes in tariffs, transfers, etc., on specific groups of productive factors within a country, these authors argue that their analysis has a perfect analogue in the analysis, within the European Community, of the effects of changes in the external tariff, for instance, on the welfare of Britain (that is, British factors of production), France, Germany, etc. This analytical approach provides, as the European Community moves to full integration, the necessary tools to analyze related issues, such as the effect of the Common Agricultural Policy on individual countries' welfare, by providing a scientific basis for calculating costs and benefits.[3]

RATIONALE FOR INCLUSION OF ARTICLE XXIV

But then, if economic theory suggests that preferential arrangements can be welfare enhancing for member countries and for others, and may therefore provide an acceptable route to GATT-wide free trade, this is not the rationale that underlay the inclusion of Article XXIV into the GATT. The theory was developed after the fact, as is usually the case, and (as is evident from the preceding analysis) even casts doubt on the preference in Article XXIV for 100 percent preferences. Why did Article XXIV then come about, and what could have been its perceived rationale?

Historical Development

As is well known, the GATT was signed on October 30, 1947 by representatives from twenty-three countries in Geneva. It was primarily a result of the wartime talks between the United States and the United Kingdom.[4] Central among the conflicts between the two countries was the tussle over Imperial Preference, which the British negotiators felt constrained by narrow national interest to rescue from the larger, non-discriminatory vision of Cordell Hull, the U.S. secretary of state under President Roosevelt from 1919 to 1944. Overriding the tussle was also the initial British worry over the balance of payments, for which Keynes, among others, wished to retain the right to engage in discriminatory practices. With his exaggerated turn of phrase, and passionate conviction in whatever he happened at the time to espouse, Keynes would write to Dean Acheson:

> My strong reaction against the word "discrimination" is the result of my feeling so passionately that our hands must be free. . . . [T]he word calls up and must call up . . . all the old lumber, most-favored-nation clause and all the rest which was a notorious failure and made such a hash of the old world. We know also that it won't work. It is the clutch of the dead, or at least the moribund, hand.[5]

However, as the United States, whose capacity to deliver immediate reductions in her high tariffs in exchange for British reduction of Imperial Preference was seriously constrained by an unwilling Congress, and the United Kingdom drew closer to their final compromise agreement in the *Proposals for Expansion of World Trade and Employment*, published in November 1945, the British economists engaged in the talks had come to view Imperial Preference as an obstacle to be removed and also to share Cordell Hull's enthusiasm for nondiscriminatory trade. In particular, Keynes would engage in one of his celebrated flip-flops by embracing nondiscrimination in the House of Lords, with as much eloquence as he had summoned when rejecting it earlier:

> [The proposed policies] aim, above all, at the restoration of multilateral trade . . . the bias of the policies before you is against bilateral barter and every kind of discriminatory practice. The separate blocs and all the friction and loss of friendship they must bring with them are expedients to which one may be driven in a hostile world where trade has ceased over wide areas to be cooperative and peaceful and where are forgotten the healthy rules of mutual advantage and equal treatment. But it is surely crazy to prefer that.[6]

The 1945 proposals were the basis for the proposed Charter for the International Trade Organization, whose stillbirth led to the U.S. move to have its commercial policy provisions incorporated in the GATT. Article I of the GATT thus embodies the strong U.S. support for nondiscrimination, while tolerating the continuation of Imperial Preference as a compromise exemption. Over time, this and other negotiated preferential arrangements would lose their value as the tariffs came tumbling down through successive Rounds.

But if preferential arrangements of less than 100 per-

cent were anathema to the United States, and ulti-
mately to the British economists on the negotiating
team, and specific exceptions were admitted into
GATT's Article I only for political necessity on a sort
of "grandfathering," "as-is" basis, the attitude toward
100 percent preferences (that is, toward free trade
areas and customs unions) was far more positive. Politically, the U.S. tolerance of 100 percent preferences
seems to have been motivated by a presumption that
European stability would be aided by economic integration and therefore the latter must be supported.
There was perhaps also an inchoate, if strong, feeling
that integration with 100 percent preferences somehow was special and consonant with the objective
of multilateralism. Thus, Kenneth Dam (1970, 274–75)
quotes the prominent U.S. official Clair Wilcox as
follows:

> A customs union (with 100% preferences) creates a
> wider trading area, removes obstacles to competition,
> makes possible a more economic allocation of re-
> sources and thus operates to increase production and
> raise planes of living. A preferential system (less than
> 100%) on the other hand, retains internal barriers, ob-
> structs economy in production, and restrains the
> growth of income and demand. . . . A customs union is
> conducive to the expansion of trade on a basis of mul-
> tilateralism and nondiscrimination; a preferential sys-
> tem is not.

A Threefold Rationale

Wilcox's statement was little more than assertion masquerading as argument. But the rationale for inclusion
of Article XXIV in the GATT appears to have been
threefold, as follows.

Full integration on trade, that is, going all the way down to freedom of trade flows among any subset of GATT members, would have to be allowed since it created an important element of single-nation characteristics (such as virtual freedom of trade and factor movements) among these nations, and implied that the resulting quasi-national status following from such integration in trade legitimated the exception to MFN obligation toward other GATT members.

The fact that the exception would be permitted only for the extremely difficult case where all trade barriers would need to come down, seemed to preclude the possibility that all kinds of preferential arrangements would break out, returning the world to the fragmented, discriminatory bilateralism-infested situation of the 1930s.

One could also think of Article XXXIV as permitting a *supplemental*, practical route to the universal free trade that GATT favored as the ultimate goal, with the general negotiations during the many Rounds leading to a dismantling of trade barriers on a GATT-wide basis while deeper integration would be achieved simultaneously within those areas where politics permitted faster movement to free trade under a strategy of full and time-bound commitment.

Tension between Intention and Reality

The clear determination of 100 percent preferences as compatible with multilateralism and nondiscrimination, and the equally firm view that anything less was not, meant that when Article XXIV was drafted, its principal objective was to close all possible loopholes by which it could degenerate into a justification for preferential arrangements of less than 100 percent.

Paragraphs 4 through 10 of Article XXIV were written precisely for this purpose. But, as is now commonly conceded, their inherent ambiguity and the political pressures for approval of substantial regional groupings of preferences of less than 100 percent have combined to frustrate the full import of the original desire to sanction only 100 percent preferences.

This tension between intention and reality has direct bearing on what I propose below in regard to strengthening Article XXIV today even beyond what its original crafters intended. Therefore I will sketch briefly the important respects in which the original intention of Article XXIV was reasonably clear but was occasionally violated in spirit, to the point where the great expert on GATT law, Professor John Jackson, has gone so far as to observe that the accommodation of the European Common Market's imperfect union in disregard of the legal requirements of Article XXIV was the beginning of the breakdown of the GATT's legal discipline, which we now seek to repair.[7] Two issues suffice to demonstrate this contention.

First, in regard to the elimination of internal barriers down to 100 percent, there was enough scope within the language of Article XXIV, paragraph 8, for its intent to be successfully avoided. Ambiguities could be exploited on two main fronts.

The first ambiguity lay in the directive that "duties and other restrictive regulations of commerce" were (with specified exceptions permitted under Articles XI, XII, XIII, XIV, and XX) to be "eliminated with respect to substantially all the trade between the constituent territories." Skillful lawyers and representatives of governments could work wonders with the concept of "substantially all the trade," and then, even if a percentage cutoff point was accepted for this purpose (for example, 75 percent of all initial trade), important issues remained ambiguous, such as whether across-the-board (75 percent) cuts on everything were required or whether substantial sectors could be left out altogether from the scope of the cuts—the latter being evidently at variance with the intent of those who favored (100 percent) customs unions but opposed (less than 100 percent) preferential arrangements. With both interpretations possible, evidently preferential arrangements could not be effectively ruled out.[8]

Next, an ambiguity of equal importance arose in regard to the problem of the speed with which the "100 percent preferences" would be implemented. Evidently, if they were stretched out over very long periods, one was *de facto* sanctioning "less than 100 percent" preferential arrangements. In GATT jargon, this was the problem of "interim arrangements." Paragraph 5 therefore addressed this issue, requiring "a plan and schedule" and asking for the customs union or free trade area to be fully consummated "within a reasonable length of time." Paragraph 7, in turn, laid down specific procedures for such interim arrangements to be approved. Needless to say, this nonetheless left the door substantially open for laxity in conception and execution of the customs unions and free trade areas under Article XXIV.

Dam's (1970, 290) overall judgment of the outcome is perhaps too harsh but is certainly in the ballpark:

> The record is not comforting. . . . Perhaps only one of the more than one dozen regional arrangements that have come before the GATT complied fully with Article XXIV criteria. That was the recent United Kingdom/Ireland Free-Trade Area, and even in that case certain doubts were expressed before the working party. In

some cases, the regional arrangements were very wide off the mark. The European Coal and Steel Community, covering only two major product lines, could not even qualify for the special regional-arrangement waiver of Article XXIV:10 but required a general waiver under Article XXV:5. The New Zealand/Australia Free-Trade Agreement, although not purportedly an example of "functional integration," provided for the liberalization of an even smaller percentage of inter-member trade. A strong tendency has also been manifested for interim agreements to provide for an even longer transitional period and to contain increasingly fewer detailed commitments for eventual completion of the customs union or free-trade area.[9]

COLLAPSE OF EARLY REGIONAL BLOCS

In any event, one can correctly assert that regionalism, in the shape of (100 percent) customs unions and free trade areas, was not generally considered, by the architects of GATT or by the United States, which was the chief proponent of multilateralism and non-discrimination, as antithetical to the GATT and to these principles.

Nonetheless, the United States, long suspicious of discriminatory trade arrangements, restrained itself from resorting to Article XXIV. The formation of the European Community in 1958, however, marked a partial watershed. The United States put its shoulder to the wheel and saw the Common Market through, negotiating around the different hoops of Article XXIV, emasculating the Article somewhat so as to seek GATT approval of an imperfect union (especially

69

in regard to discriminatory preferences for the eighteen ex-colonies in Africa that the Europeans insisted on retaining, requiring therefore a waiver of GATT rules), all in the cause of what it saw as a *politically* beneficial union of the original six nations that formed the Community. This, in fact, accounts for why, despite the enthusiasm of Harry Johnson (1965) and others for a North Atlantic Free Trade Area (NAFTA), and even a Pacific Free Trade Area (PAFTA), nothing came of it: The United States remained indifferent to such notions.

If the United States–centered proposals for free trade areas were largely patterned on the European Community's less demanding neighbor, the European Free Trade Association (EFTA),[10] there was an outbreak of such proposals in the developing countries as well. While stimulated by the European examples, they were motivated by the altogether different economic rationale formulated by Cooper and Massell (1965a, 1965b) and Bhagwati (1968) that I noted earlier. This was that, given any targeted level of import-substituting industrialization, the developing countries, with their small markets, could reduce the cost of this industrialization by exploiting economies of scale through preferential opening of markets with one another.

By the end of the 1960s, however, the attempts at forming regional free trade areas and customs unions along these lines had also collapsed. The problem was that, rather than use trade liberalization and hence prices to guide industry allocation, the developing countries attempting such unions sought to allocate industries by bureaucratic negotiation and tie trade to such allocations, putting the cart before the horse and killing the forward motion.[11]

Thus, while the world was indeed filled in the 1960s with proposals for NAFTA, PAFTA, LAFTA (the Latin American Free Trade Area), and ever more, until one could be forgiven for imagining that a veritable chemical revolution had broken out, regionalism had virtually died by the end of the decade, except for the original European Community and EFTA.

REGIONALISM REDUX

The revival of the Article XXIV variety of regionalism today, in this historical perspective, raises two questions: Will today's regionalism die, as the earlier, equally dramatic one did? And why is regionalism feared today as a threat to the GATT?

Will It Last?

That the current rise of regionalism is likely to endure and gain in strength seems probable: History is unlikely to repeat itself. There are several reasons for this.

The conversion of the United States, hitherto an abstaining party, to Article XXIV, with its free trade arrangements with Israel and, more important, with Canada represents a change of considerable importance. The United States is widely perceived as a major player, and also as the leading pro-GATT player in the postwar period, and its changed attitude on Article XXIV is a major event that shifts the balance of forces toward regionalism, as compared with the situation in the 1960s.

This shift has taken place in the context of a growing perception in the Congress that the GATT is inadequate and the "regional card should be played" as a threat to those who will not move fast enough to change the GATT to suit America's desires and interests. Since the process of change at the GATT is necessarily going to be slower than American impatience would dictate, the regional card is likely to be played again and again, reinforcing the American shift in policy.

Europe 1992 and the impending integration of Eastern Europe into the European Community have reinforced, the way the formation of the Common Market in 1959 did with many then, those in North America who feel that a countervailing bloc must be formed there as well. Indeed, the fear that European investments will be diverted to Eastern Europe, once it is integrated with the European Community, was cited by President Salinas of Mexico recently as a factor decisively pushing him toward the Mexico-U.S. free trade agreement: This would enable Mexico to get the needed investment from America, he felt.

There are strong noneconomic, political and cultural factors also driving Mexico toward a free trade area with its northern neighbor. Just as the Turks since Ataturk have tried to seek a European rather than an Arab identity, the Mexicans clearly seek now an American future rather than one with their southern neighbors. The Hispanic destiny that many in America fear from illegal immigration and integration with Mexico has its flip side in the American destiny that Mexico's reforming elite, trained in the top universities in the United States, hopes for.

The offer in June by President Bush to get more nations from South America to join the United States in a free trade area, as part of a general package of economic initiatives to assist these nations, is reflective of the compulsions that the debt crisis there imposes on

American policy to respond in a regional framework to ensure that this crisis remains manageable and does not engulf the United States, whose banks are principally endangered by it.

Finally, the conjunction of the two dramatic events, Europe 1992 and the U.S.-Canada Free Trade Arrangement, even though fortuitous and prompted by wholly different motivations and historical circumstances, certainly has created a sense elsewhere that regionalism is the order of the day and others must follow suit. In the Far East, for instance, there has been a sense that a Japan-centered regional bloc may be necessary in a bloc-infested world, though it is hard to see how one will eventually emerge.

Will It Undermine the GATT?

But if regionalism is likely to endure this time, the perception that it will undermine the GATT is also different from the perception in the 1960s that it was generally compatible with, rather than antithetical to, the GATT.

This fearful perception arises from two different sources. There is the fear that, as in the witticism about the American President who couldn't walk and chew gum at the same time, the preoccupation with Europe 1992, with the U.S.-Canada Free Trade Agreement, and with their respective extensions, will take the attention of the major players, the United States and the European Community, away from the Uruguay Round and its critical task of remaking the GATT. But there is little evidence that the feared neglect of the Uruguay Round has occurred.

There is, however, more substance to the fear that the repeated American "strategic" argument that regionalism (and agreements among like-minded nations) would be America's new weapon if GATT were not amended and bent to American demands for reconstitution and reform, combined with actual resort to regional arrangements, will produce the negative perception that regionalism is antithetical to the GATT and that proliferation of Article XXIV-sanctioned free trade areas is somehow the nemesis of the GATT. This false antithesis certainly prompted Thurow's folly in calling our attention to a live corpse.

NEEDED INITIATIVES

Nonetheless, since the impression has spread that the regional free trade areas and unions are fragmenting the world economy, instead of progressively unifying it along with the multilateral initiatives, and that the GATT is therefore being sidelined, it is necessary that the older, and wiser, perspective be restored by confidence-building measures. Among them should be the following.

Regional Structures; GATT Governance

A forceful statement must be made by the major players (through G-5, G-7, and other institutions) that regionalism and the GATT are not incompatible and that the GATT remains the central institution overseeing issues of world trade policy, despite regional blocs, much as the IMF remains the central institution overseeing issues of world macroeconomic and exchange rate policy despite the EMS and the World Bank is the premier developmental institution despite the regional banks.

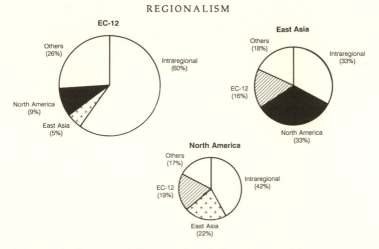

Figure 6. Shares of Intraregional Exports and Exports to Other Regions in EC-12, North America, and East Asia: 1988.

Source: GATT and International Monetary Fund; compiled by Jeffrey Schott.

Note: The exports of EC-12, North America, and East Asia totaled $1,064.7 billion, $466.0 billion, and $593.9 billion, respectively. North America includes United States, Canada, and Mexico.

Interregional Focus

An emphatic declaration must be made that international trade among the regions where regionalism has occurred and between them and other regions remains substantial and of central importance in the world economy (as is evident in Figure 6, which shows the relative shares of intraregional and external trade for the three major regions: the European Community, North America, and East Asia) and that the GATT rules and disciplines to shape it remain as important now as before the growth of new regional groupings under Article XXIV.

Strict Interpretation for New Areas

A strict interpretation of Article XXIV in regard to all newly emerging and prospective free trade areas must be insisted upon so that less demanding preferential and discriminatory arrangements do not multiply in the present proregionalism climate.

Tariff Limitations

Article XXIV also needs to be reinforced greatly in regard to its provision, in paragraph 5, concerning the requirement for customs unions, which must have a common external tariff, that this common tariff "shall not on the whole be higher or more restrictive than the general incidence of the duties and regulations of commerce applicable ... prior to the formation of such union." For free trade areas, the rule is that the "duties and other regulations of commerce" are not to be "higher or more restrictive" than those previously in effect.

Evidently, when tariffs change, as in customs unions requiring a common external tariff, and some increase while others fall, the scope for skulduggery arises again, since Article XXIV leaves the matter wholly ambiguous. As Dam (1970, 217) notes: "These ambiguities plagued the review by the CONTRACTING PARTIES of the EEC Treaty of Rome. The Six, having used an arithmetic average, refused to discuss the best method of calculation, because in their view paragraph 5 did not require any special method." Evidently, Article XXIV must be reinterpreted strictly to ensure that other GATT members are not harmed by the union or by the free trade area.

The greatest danger today is that regional free trade

76

areas will multiply, with high-tariff or high–trade bar-rier countries (for example, Argentina) being em-braced by other countries (for example, the United States), causing trade diversion that will harm world efficiency and also harm other GATT members, whose trade will be diverted to less efficient members of the free trade area. This is what makes regionalism partic-ularly antithetical to the GATT's principles and objec-tive of worldwide freer trade.[12]

The way out of this danger, which would make re-gionalism more consonant with GATT, would be to insist that any country that joins a free trade area must simultaneously reduce its external tariffs for all GATT members. A simple way to do this could be to modify Article XXIV to rule out free trade areas with diverse tariffs by members and to permit only customs unions with common external tariffs. With most tariffs bound, this would ensure that for the most part a substantial downward shift in tariffs would be a consequence— that Argentina would be lowering her tariffs, *not* that the United States would be raising hers. A surer but more heavy-handed way to ensure this would be to write in the requirement that the lowest tariff of any union member on an item before the union must be part of the common external tariff.

Openness to New Membership

Equally important, it is necessary to build a commit-ment into Article XXIV to look favorably at accepting new members into a union (or free trade area, if not ruled out by the adoption of the immediately preced-ing proposal), so that these arrangements more read-ily serve as building blocks of, rather than stumbling blocks to, GATT-wide free trade.[13]

IMPORTANCE OF THE URUGUAY ROUND

When Article XXIV was drafted, during the Second World War, its architects could not have foreseen fully either its inadequacies, as revealed by subsequent experience in the period since the Treaty of Rome, or its importance, as emerging in the last decade. It is manifest, however, that its design is inadequate to today's tasks. Its redesign must clearly get on to the ongoing agenda of revitalizing and refashioning the GATT that was launched in the Tokyo Round, is continuing with the Uruguay Round, and will certainly extend into the decade ending this millenium.*

Of equal importance at this juncture is also the task of reconstructing the GATT at the Uruguay Round. The European Community and the U.S.-Canada Free Trade Agreement have made notable progress toward extending GATT-type, fix-rule discipline to neglected areas such as services. The perception has therefore grown that the GATT is not where the "action" is. Not all action need be at the GATT, of course. But if the changes in the world economy that have resulted in major new trade flows, as with services, are not accommodated in the GATT framework of disciplines, traditionally confined to goods, the GATT will shrink in importance and fall out of view as attention to major new issues is forced into other institutions and channels. The GATT will not die; it will just wind up in an old people's home, comfortable in Geneva but uncomfortable in the neglect and inattention afflicting it.

* Article XXIV is not on the Uruguay Round, since the considerations I have outlined here were not on anyone's mind when the Round was launched. Evidently, the omission is a serious matter.

The Uruguay Round is thus of central importance. The opportunity it presents must be seized; its promise must be realized. How then can we bring it to a successful conclusion?

PART TWO

RECONSTRUCTING THE GATT:
THE PROMISE

CHAPTER SIX

The Uruguay Round and Beyond

THE Uruguay Round, begun in the fall of 1986, is now coming to a close at the end of 1990. It seeks to extend the GATT discipline to new sectors (for example, agriculture and services), improve it in the old sectors (for example, textiles), reexamine old issues (for example, safeguards protection), and embrace new issues (for example, intellectual property protection and foreign investment). In many ways, as the fifteen negotiating committees work their way,[1] the contracting parties at the GATT are engaged on arguably the most ambitious and challenging task of constitution making since the original GATT itself.

I cannot hope to address and assess here the myriad issues before the Uruguay Round; in any case, that task would strain the scholarship of any expert in international trade. Instead, I shall seek to rise above the trees and look down at the forest, posing and answering the question that is now uppermost in our minds: What could be the nature of the deal that may finally be cut?

The core areas on which the agreement must be reached are those that the main players have declared to be such. They provide therefore the jigsaw puzzle pieces that must be fitted together in an agreement in principle if the ministers are to reach a meaningful finale, as against a mere facade masquerading as success, in December 1990.[2]

These core areas certainly include the new sector, services; the old sectors, textiles (the MFA) and agriculture; the new issues, trade-related intellectual property and foreign investment measures (TRIPs and TRIMs); and the old issues, chiefly safeguards protection.[3]

THE OLD BARGAINING MODEL— SWAPPING ACROSS SECTORS AND ISSUES

Leaving aside, for the moment, the thorny and critical issue of getting the European Community to move on agriculture, let me turn to the other main issue of the overall bargain. The conventional view has been that the main bargain should be struck by the developing countries' offering the developed (OECD) countries concessions in the new sectors and issues (chiefly by accepting disciplines in services, TRIMs, and TRIPs) and trading them for concessions in the old sectors (chiefly, by dismantling the MFA and liberalizing agriculture).[4]

This model of the bargain presupposes that bargains can be cut across old and new, often diverse sectors and issues: a virtue asserted by developed-country officials in the context of the Uruguay Round but denied as illusory and unrealistic by their predecessors when the developing countries used exactly the same argument to broaden the now-defunct Global Negotiations on North-South issues. It also presupposes that the developing countries will agree to major concessions in new areas that have *either* other acutely difficult nontrade dimensions (as with banking services, for example, which raise questions of control over one's infrastructure) *or* trade dimensions that are almost unimportant and tangential (as with TRIMs and surely with TRIPs). The early opposition of many developing countries to include therefore these items at all on the GATT agenda, and the continued hesitation of some among them (reflecting probably a more widespread, if muted, sentiment), suggests that a final deal may fail to materialize if it is sought within the conventional scenario.

AN ALTERNATIVE MODEL— MULTIPLE TIERS OF AGREEMENT

If such an agreement materializes, I would welcome it. But if the negotiations flounder, I would suggest a rather different way of putting the deal together, which the developing countries should find attractive and which nonetheless offers the developed countries substantial gains, seen in the appropriate longer perspective. I would suggest that the bargain be struck on the basis of a multitiered model utilizing two distinct approaches: (1) Instead of seeking trade-offs between new and old sectors and issues, strike a bargain (as can be done) within goods, the traditional province of the GATT; and (2) on the new issues, especially services, TRIPs, and TRIMs, take a flexible approach, with these issues firmly embedded in the new GATT constitution but with different layers of commitments and rights for each issue. This approach, if I read him correctly, is consonant with what John Jackson has recently proposed. Let me explain.

Goods

The "systemic" issues in goods, which impede freer and disciplined trade, are different for the developing and the developed countries.

Most developing countries have hidden, explicitly or implicitly, behind Article XVIII(b) of the GATT, using trade restrictions abundantly to "protect" their balance of payments (and also to support their industries). But it is pretty obvious that there is no way in which access to their markets can be guaranteed, in conformity with the basic tenets of the GATT fix-rule system, if they do not learn to manage their balance of payments without resort to exchange controls and by resort instead to the standard macroeconomic policy instruments, such as exchange rates and fiscal, monetary, and incomes policies. Article XVIII(b) is based on theory that is obsolete; it also condones practice that undermines the possibility of well-defined market access to the developing countries. In consequence, as Martin Wolf has graphically complained, the member developing countries have enjoyed GATT rights (of access to others' markets) but accepted no obligations. A new GATT constitution should surely see that Article XVIII(b) be removed, or at minimum its force significantly moderated, so as to free up access to the developing country markets for goods.[5]

But, the matching systemic failure in goods trade that afflicts the developed countries is altogether different and instead relates to (1) the effective exclusion of agriculture from the GATT since America first obtained a waiver in 1955; (2) the continuing Multi-Fiber Arrangement (MFA) restrictions on trade in textiles; and (3) the occasional use of VERs and other forms of "high track" protection that bypass and violate the discipline and nondiscrimination embodied in Article XIX of the GATT. All three lapses add up to a systemic failure against the interests of the developing countries that qualifies, as Wolf is fully aware, the claim that the developing countries enjoy GATT rights in unimpaired form.

A bargain *within* goods, the conventional province of the GATT, can therefore be proposed that offers substantial, mutual gains to both developing and developed countries. The former would trade in the license permitted by Article XVIII(b); the latter would move on dismantling the MFA, liberalizing agriculture, and accepting Article XIX discipline. Huge gains in trade and welfare await such a balanced bargain.

New Sectors and Issues

But what about the new sectors and issues? The flexible, different-layers approach that I would recommend to make progress on them can be illustrated by reference to the three major areas of concern: services; intellectual property; and TRIMs.

Take services. Recall that the "middle-power" developing countries, such as India (and Brazil, until the latest presidential change, which may not endure if the past is any guide), have serious reservations about freeing up services according to a rules-based, GATT-type system. They feel that their banks and insurance companies, for instance, would collapse, leaving their infrastructure in foreign hands. Since the question of foreign investment is also tied into this question insofar as the "right to establish" is involved in many services, the matter raises also traditional issues of sovereignty that afflict questions of investment (and immigration). In short, the question is far more complex than simple trade issues are. Given this fact, these developing countries have opposed the inclusion of a services compact within the GATT for fear that complex matters there will be treated as more simple trade matters are at the GATT. On the other hand, it does make sense to have the GATT augmented to include services. How do we reconcile these positions?

My view, expressed in a *Financial Times* op ed article last year (with Andre Sapir), is that a possible reconciliation lies in going for a two-step compact on services.[6] The compact would initially extend unconditional MFN to the developing countries, with no rules obligations. But two important exceptions to the conventional rules on goods would apply and provide the compromise. The unconditional MFN rights, without rules obligations, would extend only for a *defined* period. At the end of the period, the developing countries would have to accept rules obligations or lose their rights. Second, during this transition period, the developing countries would have to accept *quantity* obligations, just as centrally planned economies originally admitted to the GATT had to.[7]

I believe that this middle approach, which addresses the concerns of the developing countries (while yielding concessions on access, now and later, to the OECD countries and keeping their central objectives and the interests of the world trading regime in full focus), is preferable to freezing them out of a services compact by "going with like-minded nations" outside the GATT or wrecking the Uruguay Round. I am happy to see that it is precisely this approach that has, in effect, been adopted by the Negotiating Group on Services in recommending that the developing countries be asked to accept rules obligations only on a "progressive" basis.

Next, consider intellectual property. The continual talk about "piracy" and "theft," which even respectable leaders of some OECD countries indulge in, when in fact the issue is one of honest differences of opinion about the socially optimal length of patents and their design (and the weight of academic economic opinion certainly does not support unambiguously the hard-line views of the developed countries on the question), unfortunately clouds the issue.[8] It is clear that the issue, which is as related to trade matters as the question of controlling the "drug trade"— that is, there is certainly a trade aspect to it but the question is far more complex—has been brought to the GATT because the interested developed countries could enforce their own views on intellectual property by using GATT-sanctioned trade retaliation. For the same reason, the developing countries oppose the matter. Again, how do we reconcile the two groups?

I would urge a different formula now. Rather than opposing the inclusion of intellectual property under the GATT, the developing countries should accept it, but with one proviso: The compact would apply *only* to those who sign it. With all OECD countries eager to sign it, and some developing countries going along with it (because of other quid pro quos in a complex trade negotiation, and other "bribes," such as indulgent debt bailouts), there is little doubt that most GATT members of importance would be a part of it. GATT retribution would cover them: They could all exclude and seize inward trade in the goods and services produced under less restrictive national patent laws by nonsignatory members of the GATT, thus covering most of what bothers the developed countries presently. Thus, for instance, India, if she did not sign, would suffer no retribution at the GATT. Nor would her own intellectual property (for example, her growing creation of software) be protected by others. The wise Jackson counsel would have prevailed, with only a subset (indeed, a very large subset) of GATT members accepting their rights and obligations in the new area of intellectual property. Over time, the reluctant countries, such as India, might even come on board.

Next, consider TRIMs. Again, as with TRIPs, these have been put into the negotiations by the United States, and now enjoy wider OECD support at the Uruguay Round, because of lobbying pressures from interested corporate sectors that see GATT-sanctioned retaliation against recalcitrant nations as a way of achieving goals that were unachievable in other ways earlier. Inserting the words *trade-related* before *investment measures* made it feasible to argue the legitimacy of considering TRIMs as part of a GATT regime. In reality, it is sensible to think of the acronym *TR* as standing not for *trade-related* but for *tangentially related*!

But what precisely are these practices that the OECD nations would like to put into the TRIMs compact that they seek at the GATT? Two are prominent in a long list, and are much the most important. One relates to local-content requirements, under which the foreign investor must assume the burden of increasing the share of locally produced components and intermediates in production. The other relates to export performance requirements, under which the foreign investor must export some fraction of production.

The problem with objecting to these practices as trade distorting and therefore to be disbarred under a TRIMs compact at the GATT is threefold. First, one is dealing with symptoms rather than the cause of these practices. Both arise in developing countries from tariffs and quotas that often reflect the failure of the developing countries to manage their balance of payments in a way that ensures current account convertibility and hence market access. The solution lies therefore in getting these countries to change their ways, that is (as I sketched earlier), to learn to live without automatic resort to Article XVIII(b) of the GATT. If a bargain were indeed struck, within goods, such that this reliance on trade and exchange restrictions were removed or substantially moderated, the frequency of the two objectionable practices would surely diminish considerably.

Second, the two practices are objectionable not only as they arise in relation to foreign investments; they distort trade equally when they arise in the use of one's own resources. Surely, the sensible thing to do, if one finds them sufficiently important to be worth bothering about, is to object to them per se rather than only as they manifest themselves in relation to foreign investment. If so, what we need is a general code, as with other codes at the GATT on procurement, etc., that restricts the use of these practices whether they afflict domestic or foreign investments. In that event, we will surely find that such practices are as widespread in the OECD countries as in the developing countries. Does anyone seriously doubt that the European Community imposes local-content requirements in a variety of contexts, for example, in considering [for critical decisions regarding trade policy] whether a Japanese car produced in Britain is British or Japanese? And who can deny that the continual Japan-bashing in the U.S. Congress, now extending to complaints about how few Americans are employed by Japanese firms producing in the United States and how much such firms still import by way of components from Japan instead of purchasing locally manufactured components, has distorted the Japanese firms' decisions to source their purchases toward the U.S. suppliers? To zero in on the developing countries on these issues, as if they were the prime offenders, via the device of TRIMs at the GATT, while conveniently bypassing the wider forms in which these practices, such as distorting local-content inducements, arise from governmental interventions and threats, is not exactly fair or calculated to produce a rationally designed world trading regime.

Third, if we were serious about removing any distortions in the process of allocating the world's investable resources, any code would have to remove both incentives and disincentives to foreign investors. Needless to say, the lobbies that drive the OECD nations to TRIMs would like the disincentives to be removed. Access to tax havens and holidays, export-processing zones that induce inflows of foreign investors and put them at an advantage against local producers, and myriad other incentives are not exactly what these lobbies would like to see an "efficient," updated GATT proscribe.

The best, indeed the wisest, thing to do would be to trim the TRIMs down to negligible size; go directly through codes to the trade practices that one wished to regulate; and let "voting with one's purse," for example, going on to Taiwan if India has too many restrictions and disincentives, induce countries to change their policies in the field of foreign investment as indeed more countries have come to do with a view to seducing foreign investors. TRIMs represent, in this perspective, a folly: a heavy-handed attempt, with little economic rationale, at trying to kick one's way into getting developing countries to accept one's presence on one's own terms.

But the fact remains that TRIMs are already at the Uruguay Round. Thus, the question again arises: How does one deal with this in an amiable way, especially as the OECD countries are wedded to the idea of getting TRIMs into the GATT? Again, the solution, as with TRIPs, is to accept them at the GATT, but to leave the membership, and the attendant rights and obligations, in the TRIMs compact up to those GATT members who wish to join.

Acceptance of this flexible approach (summarized and compared to the old one in Tables 2 and 3) will require creative leadership from all the negotiators, most of all from the developing countries and certainly from the United States, where the lobbies pushing for more radical concessions and possibly opposed to compromise are more active in trade policy formulation than in the other OECD countries.

TABLE 2
The Conventional View of the Final Deal

RECEIVE	GIVE	
	Developing Countries	Developed Countries
Developing Countries		1. Safeguards (Article XIX) 2. MFA (Textiles) 3. Agriculture
Developed Countries	1. Services 2. TRIPs 3. TRIMs	

Note: The picture above is broad and heuristic. In practice, the benefits and "costs" of the concessions cut across countries in the two groups; for example, concessions on agriculture will benefit the United States and harm some importing developing countries.

93

TABLE 3
A Multitiered Flexible Approach to the Final Deal

Tier I: *On Goods*

RECEIVE	GIVE Developing Countries	Developed Countries
Developing Countries		1. Safeguards
		2. MFA
		3. Agriculture
Developed Countries	Balance-of-payments discipline and give effective market access by moderating or deleting Article XVIII(b)	

Tier II: *On Services*

RECEIVE	GIVE Developing Countries	Developed Countries
Developing Countries		Time-bound, unconditional MFN
Developed Countries	1. Quantity obligations during this period	
	2. Conditional MFN at end of period	

Tier III: *On TRIPs*
The new compact extends rights and obligations only to those who join it. The compact is under GATT, but GATT sanctions apply only to those who join the compact. All OECD and several developing countries can be expected to join at the outset.

Tier IV: *On TRIMs*
Approach similar to that with TRIPs.

Note: The time period and the extent of obligations would differ by country and by sector, under Services.

POLITICAL CONSIDERATIONS

The success of the Uruguay Round will also require that the key components of the deal, whether along the conventional lines or the different approach I have sketched, be accepted and that the political will be mustered to implement the difficult decisions. This applies with particular force to the question of foot-dragging by the European Community on the agricultural question. Admittedly, the American demands have been holistic, seeking commitment to a zero-intervention option when even the beginning is fraught with political difficulties. On the other hand, there is simply no excuse for the impossibly slow progress on an action plan for meaningful compromise by the Community on this key issue. At the same time, the political skills of both the Community and the United States are likely to be tested sorely by the problem of getting MFA down the road of ultimate dissolution in the face of tough opposition.[9]

But Japan should not escape without admonition and exhortation. The Japanese experience that I detailed earlier, of managing trade bilaterally since the 1930s in a world hostile to her trading success, has left her with a trader's mentality rather than an architect's ambition. Weak in strength, but formidable in her powers of disruption, Japan has traditionally behaved like traders who take the rules as given and maximize their advantage as best they can. She has acquired the habit of acquiescing in quantitative limits on her exports and settling trade disputes with panicky trade partners in smoke-filled rooms. But now she has the economic strength to go beyond such management of her trade problems and begin playing a major role in sustaining and strengthening the *system*. She can lend her strength actively to the progressive forces, such as the U.S. administration, which seeks, handicapped now by domestic skepticism and even occasional congressional hostility, to make the Uruguay Round a success. Undoubtedly, bilateral management of her unavoidable trade issues, as in the SII negotiations with the United States, is inevitable. But it needs now to be combined increasingly with role-playing at the GATT. In fact, for an economy whose success is attributable in no small measure to her ability to exploit the world's markets, the counsel to play such a role is not merely an appeal to her altruism but also entirely consonant with her self-interest—as, in fact, was the case for the United States, and so manifest to those in America who allied themselves to the cause of the GATT, in the postwar period.

BEYOND THE URUGUAY ROUND

The promise of the Uruguay Round is so considerable, and the downside from its failure would be so unfortunate, that it is hard to see an agreement not finally emerging. But the task of selling it as a success, holding at bay the threats I sketched at the outset, may be yet more arduous than the achievement of an agreement. The Uruguay Round will have to be judged successful, in large part, simply if it gets the constitutional rules written on the new areas and disciplines: The process of moving on their application will follow later. The Round will therefore have to be judged as a process being set in motion, not as a termination of the process. This may well pose a real problem in the United States, where the administration must cope with tight schedules and large demands set by militant lobbies and their legislative allies with their cries of "This is what I want; right now; or else." In economics, we teach the virtues of investment, the rewards of patience. Perhaps the U.S. administration, the most progressive and powerful force in support of the Uruguay Round, will be able to persuade its constituents not to forget that lesson.

But a further worry comes from an unlikely source: from the friends of the GATT, not its foes. The recent, important work of Professor John Jackson (1990) on what an efficient, full-bodied World Trade Organization (WTO) would look like has suddenly taken wing and, supported by several governments, with Canada in the lead, the WTO proposal has attracted even ministerial attention.

All this is fine and good in theory. But surely one cannot suppress the thought that our hands are already full and our backs overburdened enough by the difficulty of bringing the Uruguay Round to a successful conclusion; the grandiose WTO task could prove diversionary and threaten the chances of the Round's success. Besides, it is surely more sensible to think, as Professor Jackson has hastened to clarify, of the GATT *evolving*, with the Uruguay Round and beyond, into the kind of structure that an architect starting from the foundations would envision. If this is not understood, there is a possibility that, while the original ITO (International Trade Organization), being negotiated around the same time as the GATT, lost out to the GATT, now we may run the reverse risk: The GATT may lose out to the WTO—a WTO whose dimensions and ultimate definition cannot be foretold except in Professor Jackson's blueprint, which reality will twist out of shape, for sure.[10]

Clarifying Conceptual Confusions and Refuting Fallacies

Economists divide notoriously because they look at different facts, or interpret the same facts differently in viewing reality with contrasting theoretical models in their computers or at the back of their minds. The problem of sorting through a multiplicity of opinions is therefore bad enough in economics, and was beautifully highlighted by that great reformer Prime Minister Robert Peel, who repealed the Corn Laws in 1846 to bring free trade to England, when he lamented in Parliament the confusions that he confronted in economics on the question. Douglas Irwin writes in a classic article on Peel's repeal of the Corn Laws:

> In looking to the economists for a clear indication as to the Corn Law's impact on wages, profits, and rents, Peel found only confusion and dissension. In an amusing passage, Peel recalled that Ricardo thought [Adam] Smith wrong on rent, McCulloch thought both of them mistaken, with Torrens disagreeing with them as well. The perplexed Peel continued [in Parliament]:

> "The very heads of Colonel Torrens's chapters are enough to fill with dismay the bewildered inquirer after truth. These are literally these: 'Erroneous views of Adam Smith respecting the value of Corn', 'Erroneous doctrine of the French economists respecting the value of raw produce', 'Errors of Mr. Ricardo and his followers on the subject of rent', 'Error of Mr. Malthus

respecting the nature of rent', 'Refutation of the doctrines of Mr. Malthus respecting the usages of labour'."[1]

But to add gratuitously to the resulting unavoidable problem for public policy by avoidable confusion of concepts and by fallacious reasoning is surely deplorable. Trade policy issues have not been immune from these problems compromising the clarity and quality of the debate.

Therefore, I examine and clarify here the principal conceptual confusions and fallacies that have afflicted us recently, and added to the comfort of the protectionists, the aggressive unilateralists, and the anti-multilateralists.

THE CONCEPTUAL CONFUSIONS

Note at the outset that international economists since the 1960s have held to the following usage, developed in the context of the postwar theory of commercial policy which made major strides in the 1960s and 1970s:

- *Domestic policy instruments* include production, consumption, sales, corporate, and factor-use taxes and subsidies and quantitative restraints. By contrast, *foreign policy instruments* (also interchangeably called *trade policy instruments*) comprise trade taxes, trade subsidies, import and export quotas, VERs and other export restraints, and now VIEs (voluntary import expansions).
- *Selective policy* means the use of domestic and/or foreign policy instruments for only a subset of sectors (or specific firms), while *generalized policy* would

100

apply to all sectors without discrimination among them.

- *Quantitative instruments* set specific limits, as with VERs, whereas *price instruments* use price incentives, as with tariffs.
- *Managed trade* means using quantity instruments, setting quantitative targets and constraints in trade. It is also called *results-oriented trade*. It is to be contrasted with *rules-oriented trade*, where quantities traded are not predetermined but emerge from the markets (with or without price instruments affecting those markets) operating under the given rules.
- The contrast is equally defined by the recent terminology *fix-quantity trading regime* versus *fix-rule trading regime*.
- *Managed trade*, or a *fix-quantity regime*, is to be contrasted sharply with *trade management*, which refers to rule-making trade negotiations and enforcement of negotiated trade rights and obligations, all of which complement, sustain and expand the scope of a *fix-rule regime*.

In the public policy debate, however, this conceptual taxonomy and other related issues have been altogether confused. The most important examples include the folowing.

Managed Trade; Trade Management

These two terms are treated in much oral and written discussion of high-tech trade policy, stemming from groups such as BRIE at the University of California at Berkeley, as if they were similar prescriptions. In fact, they are diametrically opposed in conception and implications for the world trading regime.

Industrial Policy

This is a phrase that is often used, but in different senses. One use makes it identical to what trade theorists call (as noted above) selective policy, which favors one or more sectors or firms, but not all. Another use, equally current, implicitly defines it as use of domestic policy instruments (often along with selectivity as well) in contrast to the use of trade, or foreign, policy instruments—for example, when an R&D subsidy instead of VERs is used to favor an industry selectively or a generalized R&D subsidy is used for all sectors that wish to take advantage of it. Because of these two wholly different ways in which the phrase *industrial policy* is (and can be) used, it would be ideal to banish it. But Gresham's law will again apply: Bad usage will drive out the good one. Thus, what one should urge upon those who use the phrase is to make clear, to themselves and then to their audience, which usage they have in mind.

Strategic Trade Policy

Then there is the saga of the word *strategic*. This word is thrown, like sand into the fuel tank, at those who favor open markets. Strategic trade policy is supposed to dictate otherwise; and its proponents gain the high ground in the ensuing debate because evidently *strategic* sounds brighter and, by contrast, one appears myopic and therefore sadly handicapped by inferior mental equipment. I have dealt with the substance of this debate elsewhere (Bhagwati 1989b).

Suffice it here to say that the word *strategic* in discussion of trade policy refers to the recent theoretical analysis of international competition among oligopolistic firms that enjoy abnormal ("excess") profits and "strategically interact" with one another (that is, the pricing and production decisions of one must consider the reactive behavior of the others, so that the game being played is like chess but not solitaire). In these cases, governmental trade or domestic intervention may shift some of those excess profits, and activity, to one's own nation and may even improve welfare. The term *strategic trade policy* may also be meaningfully applied, however, even in the case of perfectly competitive firms, to a government's use of trade policy, as in a poker game, in the shape of threats, confrontations, exit from negotiations, etc., to extract yet more gains from trade from other nations and even to drive bargains that leave others immiserized relative to autarky (as Nazi Germany and Stalin's Soviet Union are believed to have done).

But such usage of the word *strategic*, in the context of trade policy to shift profits to oneself in oligopolistic market structures[2] or in the alternative context of the use of trade policy to extract extra gains from trade through concessions earned in interacting negotiations with trading partners, must be contrasted sharply with the wholly different and conventional uses of the the word *strategic* as applied to industries or economic activities that politically are considered to be at the "commanding heights of the economy" *or* economically are considered to have significant external economies. There is absolutely no necessary reason for industries that are "strategic" under the latter definitions to also be candidates for "strategic" trade policy because they are oligopolistic as well. And yet, the distinction is commonly blurred.

The confusion in the literature has arisen because most laypeople, who nonetheless want to talk about trade policy whether they are economists or not, do not understand the strategic trade theory to begin with. It has resulted also because, when the same word is used in two (or more) contexts that are analytically different but can give one answers that point in the same desired direction, sloppiness often takes over. But once again, the distinguished academic proponents of strategic trade theory (who are surely familiar with the necessary distinctions) have encouraged this fuzziness by talking somewhat loosely about the strategic trade theory's being important because of both oligopolistic market structure (which is true) and externalities (which is false).[3]

FALLACIES

I will now proceed from the confusions to the fallacies that serve to undermine the case for open markets and for multilateralism. I will draw on recent writings that have received some attention in Congress and from the media in the United States. I will consider the fallacies concerning the GATT first, and then the fallacies concerning the theory of commercial policy.

Fallacies about the GATT

Several fallacies about the GATT are in currency today. I shall consider here only the following egregious errors, taken from a recent Eastman Kodak–sponsored pamphlet, which has been circulated with some success among the antimultilateral and prounilateralism circles by that corporation.[4] The errors are gross and could have been ignored. But, coming from the reputed authors of this pamphlet, they need correction at a time when GATT-bashing is a populist pastime that can prosper on any evidence, however flawed, that economic expertise is against the GATT.

> *Fallacy 1*: "The GATT forbids permanent import quotas, but says nothing about export restrictions."[5]

This is wrong. Article XI of the GATT begins: "No prohibitions or restrictions other than duties, taxes, or other charges, whether made effective through quotas, import or export licenses or other measures, shall be instituted or maintained . . . on the importation . . . or on the exportation or sale for reexport of any product. . . ."[6]

> *Fallacy 2*: "Countries are free to violate the spirit as long as they adhere to the letter [of the GATT]." And "the GATT polices what nations claim *de jure* to be doing, not what they may be up to *de facto*."[7]

Finger's (1989) response is decisive and needs to be quoted in full:

> This also is wrong. The GATT's negotiating history demonstrates that the persons who negotiated the agreement were very aware that, with a bit of imagination, a country could find ways to restrict trade that would not be covered by the GATT's stated limits, however the limits on policy actions were worded.

> It would not do, then, to limit the "policing" or "dispute-settlement" provisions of the GATT to instances in which a country had imposed a policy or taken an action that the GATT specifically prohibited. Instead, the GATT bases its dispute-settlement procedures on the concept of *nullification or impairment* of any *benefit* the complaining country might expect under the agreement. And

the GATT specifically provides for complaints about "non-violational" nullification and impairment. The relevant GATT wording (from Article XXIII) is as follows: "If any contracting party should consider that any benefit accruing to it directly or indirectly under this Agreement is being nullified or impaired or that the attainment of any objective of the Agreement is being impeded as the result of

    (a) the failure of another contracting party to carry out its obligations under this Agreement, or

    (b) the application by another contracting party of any measure, whether or not it conflicts with the provisions of this Agreement, or

    (c) the existence of any other situation . . ."

In short, not only did the GATT's formulators recognize that clever ways might be found to violate the GATT's "spirit" without specifically violating any "letter", they gave complaints about such situations full standing in the GATT's dispute-settlement procedures.[8]

Fallacy 3: "The GATT regulates policies that occur at the border . . . the underlying assumption is that . . . [border] policies can be clearly distinguished from domestic policies that may also have effects on trade." In the same spirit, "[b]ecause [Japan's fifth-generation computer program] does not tax, subsidize or restrict at the border, it does not fall under GATT rules."[9]

Finger's response may again be quoted:

In fact, the persons who formulated the GATT were well aware that any liberalization of trade-

106

policy instruments could readily be undone by "internal" instruments. Hence there is Article III, entitled "National Treatment on Internal Taxation and Regulation". The article begins: "The contracting parties recognize that internal taxes ... laws, regulations and requirements ... should not be applied to imported or domestic products so as to afford protection to domestic production." The nullification or impairment article provides the mechanism for bringing such action before the GATT "court."[10]

And one might well ask these authors whether they ever heard of the momentous preoccupation at the GATT with NTBs since the Kennedy Round's successful conclusion, as typified by the Tokyo Round codes on procurement, and so on. Evidently, familiarity breeds contempt, but contempt does not breed familiarity.

Theoretical Fallacies

The fallacies concerning the GATT are gross and inexcusable. The fallacies regarding the theory of commercial policy, on the other hand, arise from overenthusiasm. While science eventually takes care of such errors, they have played into the hands of the economically untutored and the lobbies that seek aid in their pursuit of sectional interests.

This is evident from the continual repetition of the erroneous claims (about what the "new" trade theory tells us vis-à-vis what the "old" theory told us), which are to be found, for instance, in the influential writings of such prominent journalists as James Fallows and Robert Kuttner, who prefer aggressive unilateralism, managed trade, and so on and find fix-rule trading regimes inadequate and even harmful to America's national interest. Thus, though one can only admire the important scientific contribution of the recent theorists of international trade, I believe it is necessary to address the more dangerous of the untenable claims that these theorists sometimes make in regard to the policy significance of their work.

> *Fallacy 1:* "[T]he case for free trade is currently more in doubt than at any time since the 1817 publication of Ricardo's *Principles of Political Economy.*"[11]

This is incorrect. As scholars of international trade know pretty well, the most serious theoretical challenge to free trade emerged in the post-Depression period, with John Maynard Keynes also deserting the ranks. The reason was obvious. The case for free trade, whether nationalist or cosmopolitan,[12] depends on market forces' reflecting genuine social costs. With massive unemployment resulting from insufficient aggregate demand, that assumption will not hold. Today, we would resurrect free trade nonetheless by arguing that macroeconomic policies should be used to create sufficient aggregate demand and free trade policy (where it can be applied as relevant and helpful) to reap the gains from trade.

> *Fallacy 2:* "In the last ten years the traditional constant returns, perfect competition models of international trade have been supplemented, perhaps even supplanted, by models that emphasize increasing returns and imperfect competition. These new models open the possibility that government intervention in trade via import restrictions, export subsidies, and so on may under some circumstances be in the national interest *after all.*"[13]

Several problems arise with this statement. First, there is a substantial body of theoretical literature since the 1950s on increasing returns, and it shows that a variety of market failures can arise.[14] These models also generate the existence and the indeterminancy of the trade pattern among identical economies, a matter that is also sometimes presented as a novelty of the developments of the 1980s. But these well-known models permit perfect competition in product markets to be sustained. The recent theoretical analyses innovate by letting imperfect competition coexist with increasing returns.

Second, it is not true that valid interventionist arguments for "import restrictions, export subsidies, and so on" had to await the developments in the 1980s in the theory of imperfect competition in product markets. In fact, the massive developments in the postwar theory of commercial policy during the 1960s and 1970s addressed countless varieties of market failure, and also "noneconomic" objectives that governments may properly have, and developed criteria by which one could recommend *appropriate* intervention, whether as trade (including export) taxes and subsidies or as domestic taxes and subsidies: The developments in the 1980s, which focus on market imperfections in *product* markets (whereas the literature in the 1960s and 1970s extended the scope to numerous *factor* market imperfections and to the constraints imposed by "noneconomic" objectives), have added a few arguments for intervention to an already vast inherited list of such interventionist arguments.

The misconception, now an act of faith among political scientists, journalists, and business schools, that "finally" we have theories that provide a rationale for intervention (whether through trade or through domestic subventions and restrictions), and that the in-

herited, accumulated scientific knowledge contributed by international economists prior to the 1980s
was irrelevant because it could not provide an argument for such interventions, rests therefore on lack of
knowledge of the subject matter of the theory of commercial policy.

> Fallacy 3: Thanks to the theoretical developments in
> the 1980s, "[t]here is still a case for free trade
> as a good policy, and as a useful target in the
> world of policies, but it [that is, free trade]
> *can never again be asserted as the policy that eco-
> nomic theory tells us is always right*."[15]

This sounds devastating, and indeed protectionists
have derived great comfort from this and other similar statements. But the argument is inaccurate on two
levels. First, the economic theory of commercial policy
through the 1960s and 1970s, and often earlier (for example, at Keynes's hands in the aftermath of the De-
pression), had already produced (as I noted) several
analytical arguments to support the departure from
free trade in the national interest. Indeed, there are
valid arguments in theory that go back to even John
Stuart Mill, for infant industry protection and for exploiting monopoly power in trade. Second, therefore,
the issue has always been not whether arguments *in
theory* can be constructed for policy interventions that
require departure from free trade but whether these
arguments apply to the *specific empirical situations* in
whose context we must consider the appropriate
choice of policy. Indeed, to my knowledge, all the major theorists of commercial policy in the postwar period were fully explicit that free trade was *not* "always
right" in economic theory, but that it might be empiri-
cally the appropriate policy to follow.

Fallacy 4: Conventional trade theory assumes static, given endowments of factors of production and therefore has nothing to say about "long-run comparative advantage." For example, the "Heckscher-Ohlin theory assumes . . . given factor endowments in each country."[16]

This contention is widely shared and is popularly supposed to drive the last nail into the coffin of trade theorists. But it is based on ignorance. One need refer the reader only to Ronald Findlay's (1970) classic article, over two decades old, on extending the Heckscher-Ohlin theory on comparative advantage to the long run in a model with endogenous capital accumulation. The scholars of international trade know that the issue is not whether there are theoretical analyses of comparative advantage in the presence of capital accumulation and technical change but rather how these analyses should be interpreted, and developed further, to inform the policy debate.

Fallacy 5: "[I]t might be worth developing [a] sector [with externalities] even if it requires a continuing subsidy due to costs that are persistently above those of foreign imports. This is an old argument, but it becomes much more attractive if the new theory is right, because the new theory suggests that the need for subsidy may be only temporary: . . . a temporary subsidy can lead to a permanent industry."[17]

But this is not a valid comment on earlier analyses. Countless theoretical models of "learning by doing" were analyzed in the 1960s in which the accrual of technical change was irreversible and was related to output or investment and hence could be influenced by temporary protection (tariffs) or promotion (subsidies), which could be set so as to maximize the net gain resulting from the eventual technical change benefit *minus* the initial cost of the protection or promotion. Proceeding from the early work of Kenneth Arrow, some of the most influential early theoretical analyses were by Murray Kemp (1967) and Pranab Bardhan (1970). These were in fact among the "staple" models to use when discussing one possible version of the classic infant industry argument for (temporary) protection or promotion. Again, therefore, the contrast drawn between prescriptions or insights from "old" and "new" science is false and adds unnecessarily to the prevalent proprotectionist popular belief that a new science has arrived that overturns the free trade bias of the old science.

Many more sloppy statements could be cited, showing how the quality of an important debate has been badly marred by the writings of ill-informed amateurs and none-too-careful scholars. But the small list of errors that I have selected for the reader's benefit, and the prior statement of clear concepts and terminology that should keep the debate from obfuscation, should go some way towards making this debate a more fruitful one.

Changes in GATT Membership since 1982

Between January 1982 and June 1990 the number of contracting parties to GATT rose from 86 to 96. The following is a list, in chronological order, of countries that have joined the GATT since 1982:

On February 10, 1982, *Zambia* succeeded to GATT under Article XXVI, paragraph 5(c);

On November 20, 1982, *Thailand* became a contracting party after acceptance of its Protocol of Accession;

On April 19, 1983, *Maldive* succeeded under Article XXVI, paragraph 5(c);

On October 7, 1983, *Belize* succeeded under Article XXVI, paragraph 5(c);

On April 23, 1986, *Hong Kong* succeeded under Article XXVI, paragraph 5(c);

On August 24, 1986, *Mexico* became a contracting party after acceptance of its Protocol of Accession;

On March 30, 1987, *Antigua and Barbuda* succeeded under Article XXVI, paragraph 5(c);

On June 17, 1987, *Morocco* became a contracting party after acceptance of its Protocol of Accession;

On August 28, 1987, *Botswana* succeeded under Article XXVI, paragraph 5(c);

On January 8, 1988, *Lesotho* succeeded to GATT under Article XXVI, paragraph 5(c);

Source: The Gatt Secretariat, Geneva.

On August 4, 1989, *Bolivia* signed, subject to final acceptance, its Protocol of Accession to GATT;

On November 24, 1989, *Costa Rica* signed, subject to final acceptance, its Protocol of Accession to GATT;

On April 27, 1990, *Tunisia* signed, subject to final acceptance, its Protocol of Accession to GATT.

Eight countries are presently negotiating their accession—Algeria, Bulgaria, El Salvador, Guatemala, Honduras, Nepal, Paraguay, and Venezuela. One country—China—is presently negotiating its status as a contracting party.

Dispute Settlement Cases
at the GATT, 1980–1988

Year, Number, and Description of Case	Date of Complaint	Complaint by/Versus	Referred to:
1980			
1. U.S.—Prohibition of imports of tuna and tuna products	January 1980	Canada/U.S.	Panel March 1980
2. Spain—Tariff treatment of unroasted coffee	May 6, 1980	Brazil/Spain	Panel June 1980
3. EEC—Imports of beef from Canada	June 6, 1980	Canada/EEC	Panel June 1980
4. EEC—Imports of poultry from the United States	September 1980	U.S./EEC	Panel October 1980
5. U.S.—Imposition of countervailing duties without injury criterion	November 1980	India/U.S.	Panel November 1980
1981			
1. U.S.—Import duty on vitamin B-12, feed-grade quality	June 1, 1981	EEC/U.S.	Panel June 1981

Source: The GATT Secretariat.

115

Year, Number, and Description of Case	Date of Complaint	Complaint by/Versus	Referred to:
1981, *cont.*			
2. EEC—Production subsidies on canned fruit	June 11, 1981	Australia/EEC	
3. U.S.—Imports of automotive spring assemblies	September 1981	Canada/U.S.	
4. EEC—Quantitative restrictions against imports from Hong Kong	December 1981 (recourse to Art. XXIII:1); September 1982 (recourse to Art. XXIII:2)	U.K. on behalf of Hong Kong/EEC	Panel October 1982
1982			
1. EEC—Production aids on canned peaches, canned pears, canned fruit cocktail, and dried grapes	March 1982	U.S./EEC	Panel March 1982
2. Canada—Administration of the Foreign Investment Review Act (FIRA)	March 1982	U.S./Canada	Panel March 1982

Year, Number, and Description of Case	Date of Complaint	Complaint by/Versus	Referred to:
1982, cont.			
3. EEC—sugar regime	April 1982	Argentina, Australia, Brazil, Colombia, Cuba, Dominican Republic, India, Nicaragua, Peru, and Philippines/ EEC States	Consultations pursuant to Art. XXIII:1
4. EEC—Tariff treatment on imports of citrus products from certain Mediterranean countries	June 1982	U.S./EEC	Panel November 1982
5. Finland—Internal regulations having an effect on imports of certain parts of footwear	September 1982	EEC/Finland	Panel established in November 1982 (matter not pursued by the EEC)
6. Switzerland— Imports of table grapes	October 1982	EEC/Switzerland	Art. XXIII:1 consultations (matter not pursued)
7. EEC—Import restrictive measures on videotape recorders	December 1982	Japan/EEC	Art. XXIII:1 consultations (matter not pursued following a bilateral agreement)

Year, Number, and Description of Case	Date of Complaint	Complaint by/Versus	Referred to:
1982, *cont.*			
8. U.S.—"Manufacturing Clause" in U.S. copyright legislation	September 1982	EEC/U.S.	Panel April 1983
1983			
1. Japan—Measures on imports of leather	January 1983	U.S./Japan	Panel April 1983
2. Japan—nullification or impairment of benefits and impediment to the attainment of GATT objectives	April 1983	EEC/Japan	Art. XXIII:1 consultations (request for a GATT working party not pursued)
3. U.S.—Imports of sugar	May 1983	Nicaragua/ U.S.	Panel July 1983
4. U.S.—Reclassification of machine-threshed tobacco	September 1983	EEC/U.S.	Art. XXIII:1 consultations (matter not pursued)
1984			
1. EEC—Imports of newsprint from Canada	January 1984	Canada/EEC	Panel March 1984
2. Chile—Import measures on certain dairy products	May 1984	EEC/Chile	Art. XXIII:1 consultations (matter not pursued)

Year, Number, and Description of Case	Date of Complaint	Complaint by/Versus	Referred to:
1984, *cont.*			
3. Canada—Discriminatory application of retail sales tax on gold coins	July 1984	South Africa/ Canada	Panel November 1984
4. New Zealand— Imports of electrical transformers from Finland	July 1984	Finland/ New Zealand	Panel October 1984
5. EEC—Operations of its beef and veal regime	October 1984	Australia/ EEC	Art. XXIII:1 consultations (matter not pursued)
6. U.S.—Ban on imports of steel pipes and tubes from the EC	December 1984	EEC/U.S.	Council
1985			
1. Canada—Import distribution and sale of alcoholic drinks by provincial marketing agencies	February 1985	EEC/Canada	Panel March 1985 (composition of panel announced in December 1986)
2. U.S.—Restrictions on imports of certain sugar-containing products	March 1985	Canada/U.S.	Panel March 1985 (matter not pursued)

Year, Number, and Description of Case	Date of Complaint	Complaint by/Versus	Referred to:
1985, *cont.*			
3. Japan—Quantitative restrictions on imports of leather footwear	July 1985	U.S./Japan	Panel July 1985 (matter not pursued)
4. U.S.—Trade measures affecting Nicaragua	July 1985	Nicaragua/ U.S.	Panel October 1985
5. U.S.—Restrictions on imports of cotton pillowcases and bedsheets	September 1985	Portugal/U.S.	Art. XXIII:1 consultations (matter not pursued)
6. EC—Ban on importation of skins of certain seal pups and related products	December 1985	Canada/EEC	Art. XXIII:1 consultations (matter not pursued)
1986			
1. U.S.—imports of nonbeverage ethyl alcohol from Brazil	May 1986	Brazil/U.S.	Art. XXIII:1 consultations (matter not pursued)
2. Japan—Restrictions on imports of certain agricultural products	August 1986	U.S./Japan	Panel October 1986
3. Japan—Customs duties, taxes, and labeling practices on imported wines and alcoholic beverages	October 1986	EEC/Japan	Panel February 1987

Year, Number, and Description of Case	Date of Complaint	Complaint by/Versus	Referred to:
1986, cont.			
4. Japan—Restrictions on imports of herring, pollock, and surimi	October 1986	U.S./Japan	Council/ November 1986
5. Canada—Restrictions on exports of unprocessed uranium	December 1986	U.S./Canada	Art. XXIII:1 consultations
1987			
1–3. U.S.—Tax on petroleum and certain imported substances	January 1987	Canada, EEC, and Mexico/ U.S.	Panel February 1987
4. U.S.—Customs user fee	February 1987	Canada and EEC/U.S.	Panel March 1987
5. Japan—Agreement Regarding Trade in Semi-Conductors	February 1987	EEC/Japan	Panel April 1987
6. Canada—Restrictions on exports of unprocessed salmon and herring	February 1987	U.S./Canada	Panel March 1987
7. U.S.—Tax reform legislation for small passenger aircraft	April 1987	EEC/U.S.	Art. XXIII:1 consultations April 1987
8. U.S.—Section 337 of the United States Tariff Act of 1930	April 1987	EEC/U.S.	Panel October 1987

Year, Number, and Description of Case	Date of Complaint	Complaint by/Versus	Referred to:
1987, cont.			
9. U.S.—Restrictions on certain Japanese products	April 1987	Japan/U.S.	Art. XXIII:1 consultations
10. India—Import restrictions on almonds	June 1987	U.S./India	Panel November 1987
11. EEC—Enlargement of EEC	June 1987	Argentina/ EEC	Council July 1987
12. EEC—Third-country meat directive	October 1987	U.S./EEC	Council October 1987
13. Japan—Imports of SPF-dimension lumber	November 1987	Canada/ Japan	Panel March 1988
14. U.S.—Tariff increases and import prohibitions on products from Brazil	November 1987	Brazil/U.S.	Art. XXIII:1 consultations and request for good offices of Director General
15. EEC—Implementation of Harmonized system	November 1987	Argentina/ EEC	Art. XXIII:1 consultations
16. Norway—Restrictions on imports of apples and pears	November 1987	U.S./Norway	Panel March 1988

Year, Number, and Description of Case	Date of Complaint	Complaint by/Versus	Referred to:
1987, cont.			
17. Japan—Copper trading practices in Japan	Joint request for concilia- tion in De- cember 1987 following bi- lateral con- sultations un- der Art. XXII	EEC/Japan	Conciliation by Director- General un- der 1979 Un- derstanding, para. 8 (BISD 26S/210
1988			
1. U.S.—Removal of GSP concessions for Chile	January 1988	Chile/U.S.	Art. XXIII:1 consultations
2. Korea—Restric- tions on imports of beef	February 1988	U.S./Korea	Panel May 1988
3. Korea—Restric- tions on imports of beef	March 1988	Australia/ Korea	Panel May 1988
4. EEC—Prohibition on imports of almonds by Greece	April 1988	U.S./EEC	Request for GATT panel under Art. XXIII:2
5. Japan—Restric- tions on imports of beef and cit- rus products	April 1988	U.S./Japan	Panel May 1988
6. Sweden—Restric- tions on imports of apples and pears	April 1988	U.S./Sweden	Request for GATT panel under Art. XXIII:2
7. U.S.—Qualilty standards for grapes	April 1988	Chile/U.S.	Art. XXIII:1 consultations

123

Year, Number, and Description of Case	Date of Complaint	Complaint by/Versus	Referred to:
1988, *cont.*			
8. Japan—Restrictions on imports of beef	April 1988	Australia/ Japan	Panel May 1988
9. EEC—Payments and subsidies paid to processors and producers of oilseeds and related animal feed proteins	April 1988	U.S./EEC	Panel June 1988
10. Korea—Restrictions on imports of beef	April 1988	New Zealand/Korea	Panel September 1988
11. EEC—Restrictions on imports of apples	April 1988	New Zealand/EEC	Request for panel
12. EEC—Import licenses for dessert apples	May 1988	Chile/EEC	Panel May 1988
13. Japan—Restrictions on imports of beef	May 1988	New Zealand/Japan	Art. XXIII:1 consultations
14. U.S.—Restrictions on imports of sugar	July 1988	Australia/ U.S.	Panel September 1988
15. U.S.—Import restrictions on agricultural products based on 1955 waiver	July 1988	EEC/U.S.	Panel June 1989

Year, Number, and Description of Case	Date of Complaint	Complaint by/Versus	Referred to:
1988, cont.			
16. EEC—Import restrictions on apples from the United States	July 1988	U.S./EEC	Panel September 1988
17. EEC—Regulation on imports of parts and components	July 1988	Japan/EEC	Panel October 1988
18. U.S.—Restrictions on products from Brazil	November 1988	Brazil/U.S.	Panel February 1989
19. U.S.—Increase in duty on certain products from the EC	November 1988	EEC/U.S.	Request for council ruling and establishment of panel under Art. XXIII
20. Canada—Import restrictions on ice cream and yogurt	December 1988	U.S./Canada	Panel December 1988
21. U.S.—Import prohibitions on ice cream from Canada	December 1988	Canada/U.S.	Art. XXIII:1 consultations

Explaining Section 301, Special 301, and Super 301 in U.S. Trade Legislation: The Instruments of Aggressive Unilateralism

CHAPTER 1 of Title III of the Trade Act of 1974, as amended, provides the domestic counterpart to the GATT consultation and dispute settlement procedures and U.S. domestic authority to impose import restrictions as retaliatory action, if necessary, to enforce rights asserted by the United States against unjustifiable, unreasonable, or discriminatory foreign trade practices which burden or restrict U.S. commerce. The broad inclusive nature of Section 301 authority applies to practices and policies of countries whether or not they are covered by, or are members of, GATT or other trade agreements. The USTR administers the statutory procedures through an interagency committee.

SECTION 301 AUTHORITY

Under Section 301, *if* the U.S. Trade Representative determines that a foreign act, policy, or practice *violates or is inconsistent with a trade agreement or is unjusti-*

Source: This simple statement of the Section 301, Super 301, and Special 301 procedures since the 1988 Act comes from *Overview*

fiable and burdens or restricts U.S. commerce, then action by the USTR to enforce the trade agreement rights or to obtain the elimination of the act, policy, or practice is *mandatory*, subject to the specific direction, if any, of the President. The USTR is not required to act, however, if (1) the GATT contracting parties have determined, a GATT panel has reported, or a dispute settlement ruling under a trade agreement finds that U.S. trade agreement rights have not been denied or violated; (2) the USTR finds that the foreign country is taking satisfactory measures to grant U.S. trade agreement rights, the foreign country has agreed to eliminate or phase out the practice or to an imminent solution to the burden or restriction on U.S. commerce, or has agreed to provide satisfactory compensatory trade benefits; or (3) the United States finds in extraordinary cases that action would have an adverse impact on the U.S. economy substantially out of proportion to the benefits of action, or action would cause serious harm to the U.S. national security. Any action taken must affect goods or services of the foreign country in an amount equivalent in value to the burden or restriction being imposed by that country on U.S. commerce.

If the USTR determines that the act, policy, or practice is *unreasonable or discriminatory* and burdens or restricts U.S. commerce and action by the United States is appropriate, then the USTR has *discretionary* authority as under prior law to take all appropriate and feasible action, subject to the specific direction, if any, of the President, to obtain the elimination of the act, policy, or practice.

---

and Compilation of U.S. Trade Statutes, 1989 ed. (Washington, D.C.: Committee on Ways and Means, U.S. Congress, Sept. 18, 1989). It has been very slightly amended to conform to the needs of this volume.

As the form of action, the USTR is authorized to (1) suspend, withdraw, or prevent the application of benefits of trade agreement concessions to carry out a trade agreement with the foreign country involved; (2) impose duties or other import restrictions on the goods of, and notwithstanding any other provision of law, fees, or restrictions on the services of, the foreign country for such time as the USTR deems appropriate; or (3) enter into binding agreements that commit the foreign country to (a) eliminate or phase out the act, policy, or practice, (b) eliminate any burden or restriction on U.S. commerce resulting from the act, policy, or practice, or (c) provide the United States with compensatory trade benefits that are satisfactory to the USTR. The USTR must also take all other appropriate and feasible action with the power of the President that the President may direct the USTR to take.

With respect to services, the USTR may also restrict the terms and conditions or deny the issuance of any access authorization (for example, license, permit, order) to the U.S. market issued under federal law, notwithstanding any other law governing the authorization. Such action can apply only prospectively to authorizations granted or applications pending on or after the date a Section 301 petition is filed or the USTR initiates an investigation. Before imposing fees or other restrictions on services subject to federal or state regulation, the USTR must consult as appropriate with the federal or state agency concerned.

Action under Section 301 may be taken on a nondiscriminatory basis or solely against the products or services of the country involved and with respect to any goods or sector regardless of whether they were involved in the particular act, policy, or practice.

In taking action, the USTR must give preference to tariffs over other forms of import restrictions and consider substituting on an incremental basis an equivalent duty for any other form of import restriction imposed. Any action with respect to export targeting must reflect, to the extent possible, the full benefit level of the targeting over the period during which the action taken has an effect.

DEFINITIONS

The term *unjustifiable* refers to acts, policies, or practices that violate or are inconsistent with U.S. international legal rights, such as denial of national or most-favored-nation treatment, right of establishment, or protection of intellectual property rights.

The term *unreasonable* refers to acts, policies, or practices that are not necessarily in violation of or inconsistent with U.S. international legal rights, but are otherwise unfair and inequitable.

In determining whether an act, policy, or practice is unreasonable, reciprocal opportunities in the United States for foreign nations and firms shall be taken into account to the extent appropriate. Unreasonable measures include, but are not limited to, acts, policies, or practices which (1) deny fair and equitable (a) opportunities for the establishment of an enterprise, (b) provision of adequate and effective intellectual property right protection, or (c) market opportunities, including foreign government toleration of systematic anticompetitive activities by or among private firms that have the effect of restricting on a basis inconsistent with commercial considerations access of U.S. goods to purchasing by such firms; (2) constitute export targeting; or (3) constitute a persistent pattern of conduct denying internationally recognized worker rights, unless the USTR determines the foreign country has taken or is taking actions that demonstrate a significant and tangible overall advancement in providing those rights and standards throughout the country or such acts, policies, or practices are not inconsistent with the level of economic development of the country.

The term *discriminatory* includes, where appropriate, any act, policy, or practice that denies national or most-favored-nation treatment to U.S. goods, services, or investment. The term *commerce* includes, but is not limited to, services (including transfers of information) associated with international trade, whether or not such services are related to specific goods, and foreign direct investment by U.S. persons with implications for trade in goods or services.

Petitions and Investigations

Any interested person may file a petition under Section 302 with the USTR requesting the President to take action under Section 301 and setting forth the allegations in support of the request. The USTR reviews the allegations and must determine within forty-five days after receipt of the petition whether to initiate an investigation. The USTR may also self-initiate an investigation after consulting with appropriate private sector advisory committees. Public notice of determinations is required, and in the case of decisions to initiate, publication of a summary of the petition and an opportunity for the presentation of views, including a public hearing if timely requested by the petitioner or any interested person.

In determining whether to initiate an investigation of any act, policy, or practice specifically enumerated as actionable under Section 301, the USTR has the discretion to determine whether action under Section 301 would be effective in addressing that act, policy, or practice.

Section 303 requires the use of international procedures for resolving the issues to proceed in parallel with the domestic investigation. The USTR, on the same day as the determination to initiate an investigation, must request consultations with the foreign country concerned regarding the issues involved. The USTR may delay the request for up to ninety days in order to verify or improve the petition to ensure an adequate basis for consultation.

If the issues are covered by a trade agreement and are not resolved during the consultation period, if any, specified in the agreement, then the USTR must promptly request formal dispute settlement under the agreement before the earlier of the close of the consultation period specified in the agreement, if any, or 150 days after the consultation began. The USTR must seek information and advice from the petitioner, if any, and from appropriate private sector advisory committees in preparing presentations for consultations and dispute settlement proceedings.

USTR Unfairness and Action Determinations and Implementation

Section 304 sets forth specific time limits within which the USTR must make determinations of whether an act, policy, or practice meets the unfairness criteria of Section 301 and, if affirmative, what action, if any, should be taken. These determinations are based on the investigation under Section 302, and, if a trade agreement is involved, on the international consultations and, if applicable, on the results of the dispute settlement proceedings under the agreement.

The USTR must make these determinations:

—within 18 months after the date the investigation is initiated or thirty days after the date the dispute settlement procedure is concluded, whichever is earlier, in cases involving a trade agreement, other than the agreement on subsidies and countervailing measures;

—within twelve months after the date the investigation is initiated in cases not involving trade agreements or involving the agreement on subsidies and countervailing measures; or

—within six months after the date the investigation is initiated in cases involving intellectual property rights priority countries, or within nine months if the USTR determines such cases (1) involve complex or complicated issues that require additional time, (2) the foreign country is making substantial progress on legislative or administrative measures that will provide adequate and effective protection, or (3) the foreign country is undertaking enforcement measures to provide adequate and effective protection. The applicable deadline is postponed by up to ninety days if consultations with the foreign country involved were so delayed.

Before making the determinations, the USTR must provide an opportunity for the presentation of views, including a public hearing if requested by an interested person and obtain advice from the appropriate private sector advisory committees. If expeditious action is required, the USTR must comply with these requirements after making the determinations. The USTR may also request the views of the International Trade Commission on the probable impact on the U.S. economy of taking the action. Any determinations must be published in the Federal Register.

Section 305 requires the USTR to *implement* any Section 301 actions within thirty days after the date of the determination to take action. The USTR may delay implementation by not more than 180 days if (1) the petitioner or, in the case of a self-initiated investigation, a majority of the domestic industry requests a delay; or (2) the USTR determines that substantial progress is being made, or that a delay is necessary or desirable, to obtain U.S. rights or a satisfactory solution. In cases involving intellectual property rights priority countries, action implementation may be delayed beyond the thirty days only if extraordinary circumstances apply and by not more than ninety days.

If the USTR determines to take no action in a case involving an affirmative determination of export targeting, the USTR must take alternative action in the form of establishing an advisory panel to recommend measures to promote the competitiveness of the affected domestic industry. The panel must submit a report on its recommendation to the USTR and the Congress within six months. On the basis of this report and subject to the specific direction, if any, of the President, the USTR may take administrative actions authorized under any other law and propose legislation to implement any other actions that would restore or improve the international competitiveness of the domestic industry and must submit a report to the Congress within thirty days after the panel report is submitted on the actions taken and proposals made.

MONITORING OF FOREIGN COMPLIANCE; MODIFICATION AND TERMINATION OF ACTIONS

Section 306 requires the USTR to monitor the implementation of each measure undertaken or so-called settlement agreement entered into by a foreign country under Section 301. If the USTR considers that a foreign country is not satisfactorily implementing a measure or agreement, the USTR must determine what further action will be taken under Section 301. The nonimplementation is treated as a violation of a trade agreement subject to mandatory Section 301 action as if it were a decision on the original investigation and is subject to the same time limits and procedures for implementation as other action determinations. Before making the determination on further action, the USTR must consult with the petitioner, if any, and with representatives of the domestic industry concerned and provide interested persons an opportunity to present views.

Section 307 authorizes the USTR to modify or terminate a Section 301 action, subject to the specific direction, if any, of the President, if (1) any of the exceptions to mandatory Section 301 action in the case of trade agreement violations or unjustifiable acts, policies, or practices applies, (2) the burden or restriction on U.S. commerce of the unfair practice has increased or decreased, or (3) discretionary Section 301 action is no longer appropriate. Before modifying or terminating any Section 301 action, the USTR must consult with the petitioner, if any, and with representatives of the domestic industry concerned, and provide an opportunity for other interested persons to present views.

Any Section 301 action shall terminate automatically if it has been in effect for four years and neither the petitioner nor any representative of the domestic industry that benefits from the action has submitted to the USTR in the final sixty days a written request for continuation. The USTR must give the petitioner and representatives of the domestic industry at least sixty days' advance notice by mail of termination. If a request for continuation is submitted, the USTR must conduct a review of the effectiveness of Section 301 or other actions in achieving the objectives and the effects of actions on the U.S. economy, including consumers.

INFORMATION REQUESTS; REPORTING REQUIREMENTS

Under Section 308, the USTR makes available information (other than confidential) upon receipt of a written request by any person concerning (1) the nature and extent of a specific trade policy or practice of a foreign country with respect to particular goods, services, investment, or intellectual property rights to the extent such information is available in the federal government; (2) U.S. rights under any trade agreement and the remedies which may be available under that agreement and U.S. laws; and (3) past and present domestic and international proceedings or actions with respect to the policy or practice. If the information is not available, within thirty days after receipt of the request, the USTR must request the information from the foreign government or decline to request the information and inform the person in writing of the reasons.

The USTR must submit a semiannual report to the Congress describing petitions filed and determinations made, developments in and the status of investigations and proceedings, actions taken or the reasons for no action under Section 301, and the commercial effects of Section 301 actions taken. The USTR must also keep the petitioner regularly informed of all determinations and developments regarding Section 301 investigations.

IDENTIFICATION OF INTELLECTUAL PROPERTY RIGHTS PRIORITY COUNTRIES ["SPECIAL 301"]

Section 182 of the Trade Act of 1974, as added by Section 1303 of the Omnibus Trade and Competitiveness Act of 1988, requires the USTR to identify, within thirty days after submission of the annual National Trade Estimates (foreign trade barriers) report to the Congress, those foreign countries that (1) deny adequate and effective protection, and (2) those countries under (1) determined by the USTR to be priority foreign countries. The USTR identifies as priorities only those countries that have the most onerous or egregious acts, policies, or practices that have the greatest adverse impact on the relevant U.S. products and that are not entering into good faith negotiations or making significant progress in bilateral or multilateral negotiations to provide adequate and effective intellectual property right protection. The USTR at any time may revoke or make an identification of a priority country, but must include in the semiannual Section 301 report to the Congress a detailed explanation of the reasons for a revocation.

Section 302(b) requires the USTR to initiate a Section 301 investigation within thirty days after identification of a priority country with respect to any act, policy, or practice of that country that was the basis of the identification, unless the USTR determines initiation of an investigation would be detrimental to U.S. economic interests and reports the reasons in detail to the Congress. The procedural and other requirements of Section 301 authority generally apply to these cases except for tighter time limits to make determinations under Section 304 and to implement actions under Section 305.

IDENTIFICATION OF TRADE LIBERALIZATION PRIORITIES ["SUPER 301"]

Section 310 of the Trade Act of 1974, as added by Section 1302 of the Omnibus Trade and Competitiveness Act of 1988, requires the USTR, within thirty days after the National Trade Estimates (foreign trade barriers) report to the Congress in 1989 and 1990, to identify trade liberalization priorities. This identification includes (1) priority practices, including major barriers and trade-distorting practices, the elimination of which are likely to have the most significant potential to increase U.S. exports, either directly or through the establishment of a beneficial precedent; (2) priority foreign countries; and (3) estimates of the total amount by which U.S. exports of goods and services to each foreign country identified would have increased during the preceding calendar year if the priority practices identified had not existed. The statute also lists specific factors that the USTR must take into account in identifying priority practices and priority foreign countries. The USTR must submit a report to the House Committee on Ways and Means and the Senate Committee on Finance listing the priority countries, the priority practices with respect to each of the priority countries, and the trade amounts estimated with respect to each of the priority countries.

Within twenty-one days after submission of the report, the USTR must initiate Section 301 investigations with respect to all of the priority practices identified for each of the priority foreign countries. The USTR may, but is not required to, initiate Section 301 investigations with respect to all other priority practices identified.

The normal Section 301 authorities, procedures, time limits, and other requirements generally apply to these investigations. In the consultations with the country under Section 303, the USTR must seek to negotiate an agreement that provides for the elimination of, or compensation for, the priority practices within three years after the initiation of the investigation, and the reduction of these practices over three years with the expectation that U.S. exports to the country will increase incrementally during each year as a result. Any investigation will be suspended if such an agreement is entered into with the country before the date on which any Section 301 action may be required to be implemented under Section 305. If the USTR determines that the country is not in compliance with such an agreement, the USTR must continue the investigation as though it had not been suspended.

On the date the National Trade Estimates report is due in 1990, and on that date in succeeding years, the USTR must submit a report which includes (1) revised total export estimates for each priority foreign country; (2) evidence that demonstrates, in the form of increased exports to each priority country during the previous year, substantial progress during each of the three years toward the goal of eliminating priority practices in the case of countries that have entered into an agreement, and the elimination of such practices by countries that have not entered into an agreement; and (3) to the extent this evidence cannot be provided, any actions that have been taken by the USTR under Section 301 with respect to the priority practices of each priority country. The USTR may exclude from the report in any year after 1993 any foreign country identified if the evidence submitted in the previous two reports demonstrated that all the priority practices identified with respect to that country had been eliminated.

FOREIGN DIRECT INVESTMENT

Section 307(b) of the Trade and Tariff Act of 1984 requires the U.S. Trade Representative to seek the reduction and elimination of foreign export performance requirements through consultations and negotiations with the country concerned if the USTR determines, with interagency advice, that U.S. action is appropriate to respond to such requirements that adversely affect U.S. economic interests. In addition, the USTR may impose duties or other import restrictions on the products or services of the country involved, including exclusion from entry into the United States of products subject to these requirements. The USTR may provide compensation for such action subject to the provisions of Section 123 of the Trade Act of 1974 if necessary or appropriate to meet U.S. international obligations.

Section 307(b) authority does not apply to any foreign direct investment, or to any written commitment relating to a foreign direct investment that is binding, made directly or indirectly by any U.S. person prior to October 30, 1984 (date of enactment of the Act).

The Negotiating Groups at the Uruguay Round

THE Uruguay Round negotiations have a structure in which the Trade Negotiations Committee (TNC) is at the apex, with meetings at both ministerial and official levels, and there are three component groups: the Group of Negotiations on Goods (GNG), the Surveillance Body, and the Group of Negotiations on Services.

In turn, the GNG has divided its task among the following fourteen groups dealing with several areas and issues, as follows:

Negotiating Group	Chair
1. Tariffs	
2. Non-Tariff Measures	

3. Natural Resource-Based Products
    Metals and Minerals
    Fishery and Forestry Products
	Mr. Lindsay Duthie (Australia)

4. Textiles and Clothing	
5. Agriculture	Mr. Aart de Zeeuw (Netherlands)
Working Group on Sanitary and Phytosanitary Regulations and Barriers	(Designation pending)

6. Tropical Products	Mr. Paul Leong Khee Seong (Malaysia) Vice Chairman: Mr. Siaka Coulibaly (Côte d'Ivoire)
7. GATT Articles	Mr. John Weekes (Canada)
8. MTN Agreements and Arrangements	Dr. Chulsu Kim (Rep. of Korea)
9. Safeguards	Mr. George A. Maciel (Brazil)
10. Subsidies and Counter-vailing Measures	Mr. Michael D. Cartland (Hong Kong)
11. Trade-Related Aspects of Intellectual Property Rights, including Trade in Counterfeit Goods	Mr. Lars E. R. Anell (Sweden)
12. Trade-Related Invest-ment Measures	Mr. Tomohiko Kobayashi (Japan)
13. Dispute Settlement	Mr. Julio Lacarte-Muró (Uruguay)
14. Functioning of the GATT System	Mr. Julio Lacarte-Muró (Uruguay)

Notes

1. Note that fix-quantity trade typically discriminates; e.g., voluntary export restraints (VERs), nonglobal import quotas, barter trade, etc., are discriminatory.

2. Cf. Bhagwati 1988. I might add that first-difference reciprocity is easy to contemplate when there are only two negotiating countries. But when there are more parties than two, and nondiscrimination is mandatory as well under the most-favored-nation (MFN) clause, one must contend with an acute difficulty. Will not the free-rider problem afflict this negotiating rule, causing an unduly slow move to free trade because countries can get something for nothing under MFN? On the other hand, if negotiations produce fewer results in consequence, that leads to smaller gains. So, how *does* MFN stack up as a negotiating rule if free trade is one's objective? The question is intriguing to analyze and it is only now, with the game-theoretic tools becoming available to analyze such bargaining questions, that trade theorists are beginning to consider the issue analytically. See, in particular, Ludema's (1990) analysis which approximates well the GATT's original bargaining techniques and produces the remarkable result that, with side payments allowed, MFN will indeed lead to free trade.

3. In turn, this would tend to undercut multilateralism as the strong move to get preferential concessions for themselves and the weak grant them at the expense of the trade with the not-so-strong.

CHAPTER TWO
THE RISE OF UNFAIR TRADE

1. One would want to allow for interventions to correct for distortions, as against those that create them instead.

2. Cf. Bhagwati and Irwin 1987; and Bhagwati 1988.

3. I mean *economic well-being* as conventionally defined by economists to reflect the availability of goods and services alone, and disregarding utility to be enjoyed from the mere existence of the industry within one's borders (as may indeed animate the high-tech supporters insofar as they feel that having production of high-tech at home is synonymous with modernity). International economists, especially Corden, Johnson, Bhagwati, and Srinivasan, have considered since the 1960s the incorporation of several unconventional, "noneconomic" objectives in their analysis of policy recommendations in open economies, establishing the precise nature of the policy intervention (e.g., tariffs or production subsidies) to achieve these different objectives at minimum cost to conventional economic well-being. See the review of the considerable literature on this subject in the text by Bhagwati and Srinivasan (1983, ch. 26).

4. E.g., Finger and Nogues 1987; Hindley 1988; and Messerlin 1987.

CHAPTER THREE
THE ISSUE OF MANAGED TRADE

1. Although many say so, the most articulate proponent of this viewpoint is Clyde Prestowitz, Jr., with whom I debated precisely this question at a panel of the annual meeting of the American Association of Business Economists in December 1988.

2. James Fallows 1989, 51–52. Emphasis added.

3. The results were reported in the *Financial Times* (1990).

4. See the ACTPN Report (1989) submitted to Ambassador Carla Hills for an influential example.

5. See Dornbusch 1989.

6. The countries invoking Article XXXV were Australia, Austria, Belgium, Brazil, Cuba, France, Haiti, India, Luxembourg, the Netherlands, New Zealand, the Federation of Rhodesia and Nyasaland, the Union of South Africa, and the United Kingdom. The dependent territories of the colo-

nial powers were automatically arrogated the exemptions under Article XXXV. Cf. Patterson 1966, 286.

7. Intraindustry trade refers to cross-country trade within an industry, e.g., Japan and the United States exporting cars to each other. The Standard International Trade Classification (SITC) data, even disaggregated down to four digits, contain however large agglomerates of items that simply do not belong to an "industry" according to any meaningful criteria for the purpose at hand.

8. The fans of *Rashomon*, Kurosawa's famous film of the story "In a Grove" by Akutagawa Ryunosuke, may know that Akutagawa was born in 1892 in the borough of Kyobashi in Tokyo to parents whose income came from the supply of dairy products to the Tsukuji Foreign Settlement.

9. Jagdish Bhagwati 1988, 128.

10. Sylvia Ostry 1990, 83–84.

CHAPTER FOUR
AGGRESSIVE UNILATERALISM

1. The current status of U.S. trade legislation concerning 301, Super 301, and Special 301 provisions is quite complex and guaranteed to keep Washington lawyers in good health and prosperity. An adequate guide to its principal features, tailored to the needs of economists and other social scientists, is contained in Appendix IV.

2. See the long quote from him on the subject in Bhagwati (1988, 26).

3. The debate is discussed by Bhagwati and Irwin (1987).

4. Other reasons for unilateralism, used by Cobden and other unilateralists, are discussed in Bhagwati and Irwin (1987).

5. Cf. my lengthy *Overview* of the subject in Bhagwati and Patrick (1990, ch. 1).

6. Cf. the seminal article of Robert Hudec, "Section 301: Beyond Good and Evil," in Bhagwati and Patrick (1990, ch. 4).

7. The deflection of Section 301 actions into an altruistic

exercise of American economic power, not intended by the Congress, has been attempted by the U.S. administration to some extent but is far from the whole story. For an evaluation of such a claim, see my *Overview* in Bhagwati and Patrick (1990, ch. 1).

8. This aspect has been explored in a splendid game-theoretic analysis by John McMillan in Bhagwati and Patrick (1990, ch. 6).

CHAPTER FIVE
REGIONALISM

1. Article XXXV has been invoked in the past, of course, to deny the immediate benefits of membership to countries such as Japan. But these instances are few.

2. The key to the Kemp-Wan result is that they, unlike Viner, Lipsey, and Meade, let the common external tariff become a policy variable that is set so as to achieve the Pareto-better outcome.

3. The Brecher-Bhagwati analysis was stimulated, in turn, by the earlier analysis of Bhagwati and Tironi (1980), which dealt with the effects of tariff change on national welfare when the country also had foreign-owned factors of production in its midst. Also see Bhagwati and Brecher 1979.

4. For a splendid account of these talks and their ultimate culmination in the GATT, see Jay Culbert (1987) and the celebrated Meade proposal for an International Commercial Union that is appended to this article.

5. Quoted in Culbert 1987, 387.

6. Quoted in Culbert 1987, 395.

7. Cf. Jackson 1969. The accommodation of the preferences accorded to the overseas territories was a particular problem.

8. See Dam (1970, ch. 16) for more details. Jackson (1969) also provides a similar perspective.

9. Footnotes have been deleted from the quote.

10. The Community involved not merely free trade but

also the elimination of barriers to the free movement of labor and capital, a common agricultural policy, etc.

11. An illuminating analysis of this failure is provided by Sidney Dell (1965).

12. Trade diversion is the major source of worry about regionalism on the part of international economists. See, for instance, Martin Wolf's (1989a) splendid analysis of the trade-diversionary sentiments of many in Europe who support Europe 1992 and his forthright critique (Wolf 1989b) of advocacy of policy to secure "privileged access" to markets for the United States through preferential arrangements that is expressed in the Kodak pamphlet of Dornbusch et al. (1989). Also see Aho 1989; and Schott 1989.

13. As it happens, some of the spokespeople for U.S. trade policy (such as the former U.S. trade representative, Ambassador William Brock) have indicated the U.S. administration's open-endedness to free trade areas with newcomers. My proposal would build this right into the GATT constitution.

CHAPTER SIX
THE URUGUAY ROUND AND BEYOND

1. See Appendix V for the tasks being tackled by these negotiating groups.

2. The formal conclusion of the Uruguay Round may well be extended by a few months, as was the mid-term meeting in Montreal.

3. The important issues of increased monitoring and an enhanced role of the GATT in dispute settlement have already made headway and are not at issue.

4. This is only an heuristic statement. In reality, the effects of key concessions will cut across developed and developing countries; e.g., agricultural liberalization will harm some importing developing countries and benefit the United States (helping U.S. producers and improving the country's overall welfare, too).

5. This proposal was formulated and explored by me at a World Bank–Thai Development Research Institute Conference on Multilateral Trade Negotiations and Developing Country Interests in October 1986 and published in the *World Bank Review* 1 (4) (September 1987), in a symposium issue carrying selected papers from the conference. The desirability of removing Article XVIII(b) has also been noted by Isaiah Frank (1987) and its working has been examined by Egelin (1987).

6. Cf. Bhagwati and Sapir 1989.

7. These quantity obligations, like the period of unconditional MFN, could vary by countries and specific service sectors, of course. I outline merely the principles of the overall service compact within which the specific negotiations would then follow in diverse sectors.

8. Some of these spokespeople are the same as those who denounced similar talk by their counterparts in the developing countries regarding the "theft" of their natural resources by multinationals during the days of the New International Economic Order. They were as right then as they are wrong now.

9. In the United States, it has often come close to capturing the Congress, as with the highly restrictive Jenkins bill, which narrowly missed enactment in 1986; but it may still be contained since President Bush owes nothing to the textile lobby.

10. This is not to deny the wisdom of Professor Jackson's remark, in a personal communication to me, in support of our thinking seriously about the shape of a WTO here and now: "[A] series of constitutional problems will be inevitably faced during the 'end game' of the Uruguay Round, and in fact resolution of these could be aided by a WTO idea. In any event, after the Uruguay Round (if it is successful) we will have on our hands in essence a 'new GATT.' The question is whether it will be well designed, or have a faulty structure which will crumble during the decade."

APPENDIX I
CLARIFYING CONCEPTUAL CONFUSIONS AND
REFUTING FALLACIES

1. Douglas Irwin 1989, 45.

2. This is the argument developed by James Brander and Barbara Spencer (1981) and Gene Grossman and Jonathan Eaton (1986) in important pioneering articles. The more accessible version is to be found, however, in Paul Krugman's (1986) excellent volume of contributed essays on this subject. It has nothing to do, however, with the alternative argument stated next in the text.

3. Cf. Krugman 1987.

4. Cf. Rudiger Dornbusch et al. 1989. I quote liberally from the critique by Michael Finger (1989).

5. Dornbusch et al. 1989, 33.

6. Finger 1989, 379.

7. Dornbusch et al. 1989, 31.

8. Finger 1989, 379.

9. Dornbusch et al. 1989, 31, 32, respectively.

10. Finger 1989, 379.

11. Krugman 1987, 131–32.

12. For analysis of this distinction, see my Ohlin Lectures (Bhagwati 1988).

13. Krugman 1987, 131–32. Italics added.

14. Any graduate-level text will have chapters on this topic, where early and major theoretical contributions were made by R.C.O. Matthews (1950), James Meade (1951), and Murray Kemp (1955).

15. Krugman 1987, 132. Emphasis added.

16. Cf. Stephen Cohen and John Zysman 1987, 276.

17. Krugman 1990, 110.

References

Advisory Committee of Trade Policy and Negotiations (ACTPN). 1989. "Analysis of the U.S.-Japan Trade Problem." ACTPN report submitted to Ambassador Carla A. Hills, USTR, February.

Aho, Michael. 1989. "More Bilateral Trade Agreements Would Be a Blunder: What the Next President Should Do." *Cornell International Law Journal*, November.

Baldwin, Robert, and Jagdish Bhagwati. 1990. "The Dangers of Selective Safeguards." *The Financial Times*, January 10.

Bardhan, Pranab. 1970. *Economic Growth, Development and Foreign Trade*. New York: John Wiley & Sons.

Bergsten, Fred, and William Cline. 1987. *The United States–Japan Economic Problems*. Policy Analysis in International Economics 13. Washington, D.C.: Institute for International Economics.

Bhagwati, Jagdish. 1968. "Trade Liberalization among LDCs, Trade Theory and GATT Rules." In J. N. Wolfe (ed.), *Value, Capital and Growth: Papers in Honour of Sir John Hicks*. Edinburgh: University of Edinburgh Press.

———. 1986. "Investing Abroad." The Esmee Fairbairn Lecture, University of Lancaster (U.K.). Reprinted in J. Bhagwati, *Political Economy and International Trade*, edited by Douglas Irwin. Cambridge: MIT Press, 1991, forthcoming.

———. 1988. *Protectionism*. The 1987 Ohlin Lectures. Cambridge: MIT Press.

———. 1989a. "A Giant among Lilliputians: Japan's Long-Run Trade Problem." In R. Sato and J. Nelson (eds.), *Beyond Trade Friction: Japan–United States Economic Relations*. Cambridge: Cambridge University Press.

———. 1989b. "Is Free Trade Passé After All?" *Weltwirtschaftliches Archiv*, 3–30.

———. 1990a. "Departures from Multilateralism: Regionalism and Aggressive Unilateralism." *Economic Journal*, December.

————. 1990b. *Multilateralism at Risk*. The Seventh Harry G. Johnson Lecture, delivered in London at the Royal Society of Arts, July 11. Abbreviated version in *The World Economy*, October 1990.

Bhagwati, Jagdish, and R. Brecher. 1980. "National Welfare in an Open Economy in the Presence of Foreign-Owned Factors of Production." *Journal of International Economics* 10(1): 103–17.

Bhagwati, Jagdish, and Douglas Irwin. 1987. "The Return of the Reciprocitrians: U.S. Trade Policy Today." *The World Economy* 10: 109–30.

Bhagwati, Jagdish, and Hugh Patrick, eds. 1990. *Aggressive Unilateralism: America's 301 Trade Policy and the World Trading System*. Ann Arbor and London: University of Michigan Press and Harvester Wheatsheaf.

Bhagwati, Jagdish, and André Sapir. 1989. "Trade-off Offers Answer to GATT Impasse." *The Financial Times*, March 22.

Bhagwati, Jagdish, and T. N. Srinivasan. 1983. *Lectures on International Trade*. Cambridge: MIT Press.

Bhagwati, Jagdish, and E. Tironi. 1980. "Tariff Change, Foreign Capital and Immiserization." *Journal of Development Economics* 7(1): 71–85.

Brecher, Richard, and J. Bhagwati. 1981. "Foreign Ownership and the Theory of Trade and Welfare." *Journal of Political Economy* 89(3): 497–512.

Caplin, Andrew, and Kala Krishna. 1988. "Tariffs and the Most-Favoured-Nation Clause: A Game Theoretic Approach." *Seoul Journal of Economics* 3: 267–89.

Cline, William. 1990. "Japan's Trade Policies." Paper delivered to Ministry of International Trade and Industry Research Institute, Conference on the World Trading System, Tokyo, May.

Cohen, Stephen, and John Zysman. 1987. *Manufacturing Matters: The Myth of the Post-Industrial Economy*. New York: Basic Books.

Cooper, Charles A., and B. F. Massell. 1965a. "A New Look at Customs Union Theory." *The Economic Journal* 75: 742–47.

————. 1965b. "Toward a General Theory of Customs Unions for Developing Countries," *Journal of Political Economy* 73(5): 461–76.

Culbert, Jay. 1987. "War-Time Anglo-American Talks and the Making of the GATT." *The World Economy* 10(4): 381–408.

Dam, Kenneth. 1970. *The GATT: Law and International Economic Organization.* Chicago and London: University of Chicago Press.

Dell, Sidney. 1966. "The Viability of Small Countries." In S. H. Robock and L. M. Solomon (eds.), *International Development, 1965.* New York: Oceana Publications.

Dinopoulos, Elias. 1989. "*Quid Pro Quo* Foreign Investment and Market Structure." *Economics and Politics* 1(2): 145–60.

Dornbusch, Rudiger. 1989. "Give Japan a Target and Say 'Import!'" *New York Times*, September 24, Business section.

Dornbusch, Rudiger, et al. 1989. *Meeting World Challenges: United States Manufacturing in the 1990s.* Pamphlet issued by Eastman Kodak Company, Rochester, N.Y.

Eaton, Jonathan, and Gene Grossman. 1986. "Optimal Trade and Industrial Policy Under Oligopoly." *Quarterly Journal of Economics* 2: 383–406.

Egelin, Richard. 1987. "Surveillance of Balance-of-Payments Measures in the GATT." *The World Economy* 19(1): 10–30.

Fallows, James. 1989. "Containing Japan." *Atlantic Monthly*, May, 40–62.

Financial Times. 1990. "U.S. and Japan Head List of Dirty Traders," February 10.

Findlay, Ronald. 1970. "Factor Proportions and the Theory of Comparative Advantage in the Long Run." *Journal of Political Economy* 78(1): 27–34.

Finger, Michael. 1989. "Picturing America's Future: Kodak's Solution of American Trade Exposure." *The World Economy* 12(4): 377–80.

Finger, Michael, and J. Nogues. 1987. "International Control of Subsidies and Countervailing Duties." *World Bank Economic Review* 1: 707–26.

153

REFERENCES

Frank, Isaiah. 1987. "Import Quotas, the Balance of Payments and the GATT." *The World Economy* 10(3): 307–17.

Hindley, Brian. 1988. "Dumping and the Far East Trade of the European Community." *The World Economy* 11(4): 445.

Hudec, Robert. 1990. "Section 301: Beyond Good and Evil." In Bhagwati and Patrick 1990.

Jackson, John. 1967. "The General Agreement on Tariffs and Trade in United States Domestic Law." *Michigan Law Review* 66 (December): 249–332.

———. 1969. *World Trade and the Law of GATT*. Indianapolis: Bobbs-Merrill Company, December.

———. 1990. *Restructuring the GATT System*. New York: Council on Foreign Relations Press.

Johnson, Harry. 1965. *The World Economy at the Crossroads*. Oxford: Clarendon Press.

Kemp, M. C. 1955. "The Efficiency of Competition as an Allocator of Resources: I: External Economies of Production." *Canadian Journal of Economics* 21(1): 30–42.

Kemp, M. C., and H. Wan, Jr. 1976. "An Elementary Proposition Concerning the Formation of Customs Unions." *Journal of International Economics* 6: 95–98.

Kreinin, Mordechai. 1988. "How Closed Is Japan? Additional Evidence." *The World Economy* 11(4): 529–42.

Krugman, Paul, ed. 1986. *Strategic Trade Policy and the New International Economics*. Cambridge: MIT Press.

———. 1987. "Is Free Trade Passé?" *Journal of Economic Perspectives* 1: 131–44.

———. 1990. *The Age of Diminished Expectations*. Cambridge: MIT Press.

Lawrence, Robert. 1987. "Imports in Japan: Closed Markets or Minds?" *Brookings Papers on Economic Activity* 2.

Leamer, Edward. 1988. "Measures of Openness." In R. E. Baldwin (ed.), *Trade Policy Issues and Empirical Analysis*, 147–200. Chicago: University of Chicago Press.

Ludema, Rodney. 1990. "International Trade Bargaining and the Most-Favoured-Nation Clause." Paper presented to Columbia University Conference on Political Economy and International Trade, February. Forthcoming in *Economics and Politics* 3(1).

Matthews, R.C.O. 1950. "Reciprocal Demand and Increasing Returns." *Review of Economic Studies* 17(2): 149–58.

McMillan, John. 1989. "Managing Supplies: Incentive Systems in Japanese and United States Industry." Mimeo, University of California, San Diego.

_____. 1990. "The Economics of Section 301: A Game Theoretic Guide." *Economics and Politics* 2(1): 45–59. Also in Bhagwati and Patrick 1990.

Meade, James. 1951. "External Economies and Diseconomies in a Competitive Situation." *Economic Journal* 62(1): 54–67.

_____. 1955. *The Theory of Customs Unions*. Amsterdam: North-Holland.

Messerlin, Patrick. 1987. "The Long Term Evolution of the EC Anti-Dumping Law: Some Lessons for the New AD Laws in LDCs." Mimeo, World Bank.

Mincer, Jacob, and Higuchi, Yoshio. 1988. "Wage Structures and Labor Turnover in the U.S. and in Japan." *Journal of the Japanese and International Economies*, June, 97–113.

Nash, Ogden. 1935. *Verses from 1929 On*. Boston: Little, Brown and Company.

Ostry, Sylvia. 1990. *Governments and Corporations in a Shrinking World*. New York: Council on Foreign Relations Press.

Patterson, Gardner. 1966. *Discrimination in International Trade: The Policy Issues, 1945–65*. Princeton, N.J.: Princeton University Press.

Saxonhouse, Gary. 1983. "The Micro- and Macro-Economics of Foreign Sales to Japan." In W. Cline (ed.), *Trade Policies in the 1980's*. Washington, D.C.: Institute for International Economics.

_____. 1988. "Differentiated Products, Economies of Scale and Access to the Japanese Market." Seminar Discussion Paper No. 288, Research Seminar in International Economics, Department of Economics, University of Michigan.

_____. 1991. "How Open Is Japan? Comment." In Paul

REFERENCES

Krugman (ed.), *The U.S. and Japan: Trade and Investment.* Chicago: University of Chicago Press, forthcoming.

Schott, Jeffrey, ed. 1989. *Free Trade Areas and U.S. Trade Policy.* Washington, D.C.: Institute for International Economics.

Snape, Richard. 1988. "Is Non-Discrimination Really Dead?" *The World Economy* 11(1): 1–19.

Srinivasan, T. N., and Koichi Hamada. 1989. "The U.S.-Japan Trade Problem," Paper presented to the Columbia University Conference on U.S. Trade Policy, November.

Tobin, James. 1978. "Harry Gordon Johnson, 1923–1977." In *Proceedings of the British Academy* 64: 443–58. London: Oxford University Press.

Viner, J. 1950. *The Customs Union Issue.* New York: Carnegie Endowment for International Peace.

Wolf, Martin. 1989a. "European Community 1992—The Lure of the Chasse Gardee." *The World Economy* 12(3): 373–76.

Wolf, Martin. 1989b. "Academics Now Advocate Trading Blocs." *The Financial Times,* October 30.

Wong, Kar-yiu. 1989. "Optimal Threat of Trade Restriction and *Quid Pro Quo* Foreign Investment." *Economics and Politics* 1(3): 277–300.